the

OBSERVATION

deck

the

OBSER

VATION

deck

A Tool Kit

for

Writers

Naomi Epel

CHRONICLE BOOKS

Manufactured in China
ISBN 0-8118-1481-5
10 9 8 7 6 5 4 3

Distributed in Canada by
Raincoast Books
8680 Cambie Street
Vancouver, B.C. V6P 6M9

Chronicle Books
85 Second Street
San Francisco, CA 94105
www.chroniclebooks.com

Design by doubleugee /
Michele Wetherbee
Illustration by doubleugee /
Stefan Gutermuth

I am grateful to the authors whose names are scattered throughout this book for sharing their secret writing strategies. I wish I could list them all because many have served as valuable friends and advisors.

Long before she became my agent, Betsy Amster encouraged me to develop this project and kept me going when my confidence was low.

Craig Hetzer, Caroline Herter, Leigh Anna Mendenhall, Julie Winokur, and Michele Wetherbee transformed these words and ideas into something of grace and beauty.

Dorothy Wall, Helen Revel, Julia Sherry, Bill Reinka, Laurie Snowden, and Karen Stanton patiently read and/or listened to countless versions of various chapters. They asked helpful questions and demonstrated the deck's value by putting the cards to work in their own writing.

Berkeley's Cafe del Sol, Caffe Strada, and Au Coquelet, and U. C.'s Morrison Library provided safe havens for writing where the noise of other people made it easier to work.

Deep gratitude to Susan Stone of KPFA and to Michael Johnson, Bill Helgeson, and Alan Farley of KALW.

Terry Gross of NPR's *Fresh Air* and George Plimpton of the *Paris Review* were sources of inspiration and great anecdotes. Their interviews, as well as quotes collected by Jon Winokur in *Writers on Writing,* greatly enriched this book. Helene Silver and Jamie Sams inspired the deck's form. The librarians at the Berkeley Public Library and Sidney Goldstein of City Arts and Lectures provided valuable help in gathering information.

I want to thank Bill and Louise Reinka and Alexandra and Albert Gautraud for keeping the business going while I focused on writing.

Finally, the people who gave me courage, love, and sustenance as I worked on this project over the years: my parents and the extended Epel clan, Ellen Ullman, Stephen Thewlis, Michael Mercil, Catherine Linesch, Rod Duggan, Dottie Leroux, Douglas Gilbert, Terry Demchak, Jo Mohrbach, Bob Cowart, Sue Mittelman, Jenny Freeman, Sue Bender, Susan Page, Sylvia Rubin, Jane Gottesman, and Clara Basile.

contents

table of

Almost every day for the past nine years I have had a different writer in my car. As a literary escort, my job has been to make sure that touring authors arrive at their interviews and signings well-fed and on time. While riding around San Francisco, various novelists, journalists, self-help gurus, and children's book authors have shared the methods they have used to find inspiration, develop self-discipline, and hone their craft.

Over time I began to take note of these methods and made up a set of three-

Introduction

by-five cards meant to jump-start my own creativity. When I was feeling stuck I'd pull a card with a phrase like *Write a Letter* or *Ask a Question* that would tell me what to do. The spontaneity of pulling cards freed me from having to be too self-directive and my writing began to flow. It was as if I had a team of skilled writers teaching me new techniques and encouraging me to keep improving.

The Observation Deck is designed to help you through every stage of the creative process by combining your own intuition with the wisdom of other successful writers. This book does not tell you *how* you must work; it gives you the opportunity to experiment with different *ways* of working and relieves you of the anxiety of having to constantly decide what to do next.

This deck can help you through one piece of writing—from conception to polished work—or it can serve as a self-directed writing course in which you create a number of short pieces.

You can work your way through the deck systematically or shuffle the cards and allow chance to determine your next move. Even if you pull the same card several times, its impact will always be different. For variety, you can pull several cards and allow the combination to create a new suggestion.

Sometimes you will pick a card and immediately know what you need to do. Other times you might go directly to a chapter in the book to find help in a specific area. If you pull a card that seems totally inappropriate, trust that you pulled it for a reason and allow yourself to experiment. Remember, the cards are not meant to change the way you write, but to provide new colors for your writing palette.

Keep all the writing you do for *The Observation Deck* in one place. This will provide a record of your progress and may prove a source of valuable material for future projects.

Share the deck with a friend or two. Create a support group for working together. The many mornings that I spent with Susan Page *(If I'm So Wonderful Why Am I Still Single?)* doing exercises and reading one another's work were instrumental in helping me become a published author. You can contact my Web site at http://www.observationdeck.com and I'll help connect you with other writers in your area. Please write to share your successes. Let me know which techniques proved most helpful and why. If you come up with new ways to use the cards, I'll pass them on to other writers.

The Observation Deck is not just a tool for writing; it is also a guide for living creatively. Not only will it help you finish the piece you've been meaning to write, it will give your thoughts a means of powerful expression and will allow you to experience the world with greater depth. I hope that you enjoy working with the deck and that your writing becomes a source of strength, insight, and inspiration.

To Julia Epel Sherry,

a woman of valour, beauty, and compassion.

News

On Monday, November 16, 1959, Truman Capote turned to page thirty-nine of *The New York Times* and found, hidden in the middle of the page, a one-column story headlined "Wealthy Farmer, Three of Family Slain." The dateline was Hokum, Kansas. Anxious to write about a world he did not know, in a way he had never written before, Capote set out for Kansas with his friend Harper "Nellie" Lee. The results of this trip and the ensuing investigation became the nonfiction novel *In Cold Blood*.

Newspapers are often a source of inspiration for writers. A small article about the attempted defection of a Russian frigate inspired Tom Clancy to write *The Hunt for Red October*. He changed the ship into a submarine and created the crew, enemy, and circumstances out of his imagination.

Joan Didion let a one-inch story in the *New York Times* inspire her first novel, *Run River*. The murder and trial detailed in the article took place in the Carolinas, but Didion, feeling homesick, transferred the events to her native Sacramento.

Robert Olen Butler created an entire collection of short stories, *Tabloid Dreams*, using headlines from *Star* magazine.

Harold Hayes, the legendary editor of *Esquire* magazine, used to tell his editors to find a story in the news and give it a different spin. Scan today's paper and see what articles catch your eye. Copy down the most compelling headlines, pick one, and then make a list of ten stories you could base on that article.

You could write several fictional pieces based on one article—the story as it was experienced by one participant, a precipitating event leading up to the story, or a dramatic aftermath. You could even place one of you own characters in the situation and see what evolves.

There are also a number of nonfiction pieces you could generate— an essay, a profile, or an investigation into one aspect of the story. Pulitzer Prize–winning journalist Edward Humes says there are always ten different stories that can be derived from a given event depending on the angle from which you view it and the elements you choose to emphasize. You could examine the situation through a Marxist lens, reflecting the decline of our civilization, or you could focus on the heroism and human triumph demonstrated in the event.

On May 14, 1996, I opened the *San Francisco Chronicle* in search of ideas. The first story that captured my attention told of six climbers who died in a snowstorm atop Mount Everest. I saw I could write a fictional piece from the point of view of a doomed climber or a nonfiction profile of someone who survived. I could write about a pregnant wife waiting for news of her husband's fate or about the rescue team digging through the rubble. I could even write an essay asking if it was worth the risk or a piece on the history of mountain climbing. There were stories to be told about sherpas, frostbite, rescue techniques, innovations in climbing gear, and the economics of adventure travel.

In the same edition of the *Chronicle* there was an article headlined "Homeless Wary of S. F. Shelters." It made me think of my friend Martin, a brilliant schizophrenic who lived for many years in a park near my home. I decided to write about the way Martin brought a group of strangers together after the earthquake of 1989. I was soon calling neighbors I'd long forgotten to learn what had become of Martin and hear how he had influenced others' lives.

Jane Smiley suggests you combine elements from two different stories. For example, she thought I might bring a man from the homeless shelter into the story by making him the brother of one of the mountain climbers. Now the piece took on a whole new twist.

You may find inspiration in the back pages of the newspaper, in the want ads, or the obituaries. You may be drawn to the business section, sports news, or society page. As you read the editorials you may discover the need to counter a particularly offensive op-ed piece. A letter to Miss Manners may trigger a story or cause you to write a different response. Noticing which articles call out to you will help you clarify what and how you are really meant to write.

Choose a story from the paper and, using it as a trigger, write for fifteen minutes without stopping. If doubts or questions come up, jot them down and keep on writing. You may discover there are aspects you need to research or different tactics you want to try. But don't let these thoughts interrupt you—get them onto paper so that your words can continue to flow.

Remember, you are not going to write a finished piece in fifteen minutes. You are simply exploring. If you find that you've started something you want to continue, keep writing.

When writing about a distant time or place, newspapers can provide valuable information. You may want to know what the weather was like on a certain day or what events might have influenced a character's life.

Historian Jonathan Spence spent hours in the British Museum pouring over the *Shanghai Shipping Times* from the 1860s while doing research for *God's Chinese Son*. Spence was scanning the want ads when he stumbled upon a series of ads for lost dogs. When he realized why the dogs were missing, he began to understand the horror wrought by the famine that plagued the land. Spence listed the names he'd culled from the ads in the famine chapter, honoring the missing pets and granting them a kind of immortality.

If you are writing about a time in the future, imagine what kind of stories the newspapers (if they still exist) might contain. Are serial killers still front page news? Where are the most important conflicts taking place? What new scientific developments are in the offing? Create a list of headlines and see what they tell you about that world.

When best-selling children's book author Jack Prelutsky is looking for a new idea, he takes a poem he's written and turns it upside down. Playing with opposites, he took a poem about an overcooked dinner, "My Mother Made a Meatloaf," and let it give rise to a poem about an undercooked meal—"The Turkey Flew Out of the Oven." A poem about a slow-moving, do-nothing dinosaur—"Brachiosaurus had nothing to do / but stand with its head in the treetops and

Flip it Over

chew"—was flipped to generate a poem about a wild ride atop a bucking Brontosaurus.

Take something you have written, or have been trying to write, and play with its opposite. If you are writing about two people breaking up, recount the moment they first fell in love. If you are trying to describe a winning catch, detail a fatal fumble. If you've been thinking about death, write about someone or something being born.

Let a scene set on a summer morning lead you to write about a winter night. Change a rural setting into an urban environment.

If you're writing nonfiction and making a case for some position—preserving a landmark, updating a theory, banning a drug—compose an argument for the other side. In arguing your opponents' case, you will discover weaknesses in their logic, the places vulnerable to attack. You will also see areas where you must bolster your own defenses. By taking on a rival's argument, you may uncover a hidden agenda, which will give you further ammunition.

Take something you've been reading and rewrite the story with a different outcome. Or change one essential element in a story. If you were to cast the witch in "Hansel and Gretel" as a man instead of a woman, how would that effect the tone?

Make your hero fat instead of thin, old instead of young, rich instead of poor. Switch the gender of one character. Turn your villain into a victim. Set a historical incident in the future, or place a futuristic story in the past.

If you are feeling stuck, play with the advice Flannery O'Connor gave upon learning that a friend's book had been rejected: "Try rearranging it backwards and see what you see." O'Connor learned to do this in an art class where students turned their pictures upside down to see what could be added or removed. "A lot of excess stuff will drop off this way."

Reverse one of your writing habits. If you normally do things slowly, write today at maximum speed. If you are a heavy reviser, pretend to be an improviser. If you usually reread yesterday's work before starting, don't do it today. If you never reread, try it. If you rarely plan your work, create an outline. If you always outline, don't.

Jog yourself out of a rut by turning things around and doing something different. You don't need to make these changes permanent. Tomorrow you can return to your old routine, refreshed.

zoom

In and Out

For novelist Amy Tan, the process of writing often begins with a single image—like a pair of chopsticks joined by a silver chain. Using her mind as a camera, Tan pulls back from the chopsticks to take in the larger picture—she sees the table on which the chopsticks lie, the dimly lit room in which the table sits, the different people moving around in the room. "I focus on a specific image and that image takes me into a scene. Then I begin to see the scene and I ask myself, 'What's to your right?

What's to your left?' And I open up into this fictional world."

Try using your mind as a camera. If you are writing about a group of people, zoom in for a close-up of one person's face or hands. Or focus on some object that lies between them.

Pull back from the scene as if you had a camera mounted on a helicopter: see the place where your characters have gathered in a broader perspective. See the house in relation to its neighborhood, the city, state, and world. Observe where the building in your scene is set. Is it in the heart of downtown? Or just off the highway in an industrial park? Is it the tallest, the oldest, the most ornate building? How does it compare to the rest of the area? How far away is it from the slums?

If you are looking for something to write about, picture an object—like Amy Tan's chopsticks—and imagine it in a different context. Focus on the item, examine it, and then pull back to see it as part of a larger scene. You might begin with a cigarette lighter and, as you pull back, notice the pinky ring on the hand that is flicking the lighter open. There is a hairy wrist just above the hand and a set of diamond cufflinks. Your eye travels up the arm and you see the man. He is lighting a woman's cigarette. They are in a smoke-filled nightclub. There is a small man watching them closely from the balcony. Suddenly you've got a story.

Novelist Jerzy Kosinski described his writing process to the *Paris Review:* "I select from the novel's master plan, from its topography, a fragment of a scene I find most inspiring at the given time, and then write it moving either 'above it' or 'below it.' Since I start with an image, let's say of a man being driven in his car through the West Virginia countryside—I might first write about the rain, or his car, or what he felt at the end of the drive, and only then confront the scene's dramatic center."

Spend some time focusing on a pine cone, a piece of glass, the bark of a tree. Get down on your hands and knees and closely examine a square foot of grass. Take out a magnifying glass and really look at a strand of hair, an ear of corn, a fingerprint. Draw or trace a pair of glasses, a stapler, a clock—to help you see details you might normally overlook.

Find a place where you can get a broad perspective of the world. Sit atop the highest hill or ride to the top of a very tall building. Feel how small you are in the larger context and enjoy the freedom this knowledge can bring.

Lines

You have a world of powerful teachers sitting on the bookshelves in your house right now. Pick up a favorite book and look at the opening lines. Who is speaking? How does the book begin? What has the author done to draw you in? How does the opening relate to the end of the story?

Let's look at a few opening lines from favorite books that I pulled off my bookshelf at home:

"To the world when it was half a thousand years younger, the outlines of all things seemed more clearly marked than to us."
—J. Huizinga, *The Waning of the Middle Ages*

"It was a queer, sultry summer, the summer they electrocuted the Rosenbergs, and I didn't know what I was doing in New York."
—Sylvia Plath, *The Bell Jar*

"My wound is geography. It is also my anchorage, my port of call."
—Pat Conroy, *The Prince of Tides*

"I can see by my watch, without taking my hand from the left grip of the cycle, that it is eight-thirty in the morning."
—Robert Pirsig, *Zen and the Art of Motorcycle Maintenance*

"In those days cheap apartments were almost impossible to find in Manhattan, so I had to move to Brooklyn."
—William Styron, *Sophie's Choice*

Some of these examples are poetic, others fairly mundane. Why is it important that Styron's narrator, Stingo, moved to Brooklyn? Is it simply because that is where he met the tormented Sophie and Nathan? Author Ellen Ullman suspects that a lesser writer might never have gotten away with such an undramatic opening, but readers are patient with Styron, trusting him to deliver a powerful story, because he has done so with each of his earlier books. Ullman points out that Styron structured *Sophie's Choice* like a spiral coil. He starts out at a leisurely pace but with each painful revelation of Sophie's past, he tightens the spring until the reader must find cathartic release.

Look closely at several of the books on your shelf. Pick one opening sentence that calls out to you. Ask yourself what makes it work. Does it grab your attention? Set a mood? Transport you to another place or time? Now, take that sentence and write your own version of the paragraphs that might follow. Write for ten minutes. Do not censor. Do not worry about creating great literature, just write.

Walter Kirn, author of *She Needed Me*, believes that the opening line of a book should give the reader a sense of how the story will end. The whole arc of the book should be implied in the opening sentence. Is this true for your favorite openings? If so, how? When looking at your favorite books ask how the first line relates to the final line. Also, what is the relationship between a chapter opening and a chapter closing? What is the writer trying to accomplish?

Before going to bed tonight, ask yourself to wake up in the morning with a great opening line. Prime the pump by writing about your work and what you wish to convey, then see what your dreams produce. You may be surprised when an answer comes to you in the shower or while driving to work.

Take a favorite fairy tale and imagine turning it into a contemporary story. Write ten different opening sentences. Pick one and keep writing to see what evolves.

Brainstorm a list of twenty-five spontaneous opening lines. These need not relate to any preconceived story ideas. Twenty-four sentences are not enough—do a full twenty-five. Write some in the style of your favorite authors. Then pick one and compose the paragraphs that follow.

Right now, as you sit here reading these words, you are surrounded by sound. Sounds close by and far away. Sounds that arise from inside your body, sounds you make as you move in your chair. The hum of electricity, the whisper of your breath, the rumble of passing cars—rhythmic tones and sustained notes are playing out all around you.

Take the next few minutes to simply listen. Close your eyes and let yourself hear the many levels and textures of your audi-

Listen

tory world. Notice how relaxed you become as you focus your awareness on sound.

Now pick up your pen or move toward your keyboard. Notice the sounds you generate with your hands and feet. Begin to write by simply listing all that you hear. Perhaps one sound will activate a memory or evoke an image of the object at its source. Let the act of listening carry you into a state of easy writing. Write without thinking for the next ten minutes. Do not stop before the time is up. Even if you feel you've said all that you have to say by minute seven, keep going.

Listening can be done anyplace and anytime. When bored with a lecture or walking alone in a park, take the time to listen and to write. While waiting for an appointment, notice the music of the office in the background. Absorb the buzz of the audience as you wait for a concert to begin. Tune in to the clatter of silver and glass while sitting in a restaurant.

I once attended a high-brow conference where simultaneous interpreters translated the proceedings from a glassed-in booth at the back of the hall. By changing the channel on my headphones, I could hear the lecture in Spanish, Chinese, or Russian. I decided that anything would be better than listening to people pontificate in English, so I switched channels and let the music of the Chinese translation take over my senses. For the next two hours, riding a wave of unfamiliar sound, I drew and wrote more easily than I had in a long time.

Sounds evoke memory and emotion. Randy Thoms, an Academy Award–winning sound designer, often mixes a number of different sounds to give sonic resonance to movie elements. For *The Right Stuff,* Thoms wanted to give the screen door of a restaurant a distinct and complex auditory character, so he combined the opening creak of one door with the oil-thirsty swing of another, and the echoing slam of a third. To add tension to a car chase, Thoms mixed in the screams of a charging elephant with the sound of squealing tires, creating a kind of auditory simile.

As you notice various sounds throughout the day, ask yourself what images a sound brings to mind. To evoke the sweet taste of plums that Michael Ondaatje describes in his book *The English Patient*, Academy Award–winning sound editor Walter Murch used the soft ringing of church bells in the distance. Allow this type of aural awareness to carry over into your writing.

When working on a scene, visit similar settings with your ears. Visit a factory, a zoo, an office, a child-filled household, a lounge bar. Record all the sounds that you hear. Even if you never mention these sounds in your story, your awareness will add richness to your understanding of the places you portray in your writing.

Listen to a sound over time. Notice how the sound begins. How does it change before fading away? Let a sound remind you of a time and place in the past. What sounds were different then? Telephones? Clocks? Sirens? People's voices?

Writing these words, I realize how many of the sounds that stir my memory are disappearing from the world. The electronic age has replaced the clack of typewriter keys with a quiet buzz. Make a list of sounds you may never hear again.

List the sounds that are characteristic of a certain season. How does autumn sound different from winter? What are some of the noises of summer or spring? Create a sonic portrait of a particular time of year.

Listen to a familiar object—a ticking clock, a revving engine, a running faucet. Create an imaginary scene involving that object.

If you are working on a scene right now, take a minute to imagine what sounds might be going on in the background. Are there voices in the distance? If so, are these voices laughing? Whispering? Arguing? What kind of machines might be heard in this scene? The hum of a refrigerator? The bell of a cash register? The music coming from a radio? Find a way to weave more sounds into your work.

I once heard actor Danny Glover say that he dedicates every performance to someone—it might be South Africa's president Nelson Mandela or the old man who guards the stage door—but he is always working for someone other than himself. This focus gives his acting purpose and makes his work rich.

Even though your first audience may be yourself, it is helpful to think of your work as a gift—whether that be creating a thing of beauty for others to see or showing oth-

Dedicate

ers that they are not alone in their pain. You may be writing to warn people of the dangers of some practice or to show them how a system works, but you are creating a work that will be useful to others.

John Steinbeck wrote the novel *East of Eden* partly to help his sons understand their heritage. "I want to tell them directly, and perhaps by speaking directly to them I shall speak directly to other people. One can go off into fanciness if one writes to a huge nebulous group. But I think it will be necessary to speak very straight and clearly and simply if I address my book to two little boys who will be men before they read my book."

Think about someone you'd like to reach through your writing. It will give your work a clearer tone and greater power.

Anthony Burgess described his ideal reader as "a lapsed Catholic and a failed musician, short-sighted, color blind, auditorially biased, who has read the books that I have read. He should also be about my age." Burgess writes books that he himself would like to read.

Gloria Naylor *(The Women of Brewster Place)* began writing because she found few books that addressed intelligent black women like herself. Of course her books crossed over to a larger audience, but she knew that the black woman's perspective was underrepresented and wanted to help remedy the problem.

When novelist Tom "We'll leave the light on for you" Bodett (of Motel Six fame) was doing his radio show from Alaska, he imagined he was talking across the hood of a car to a friend of his who had died. Listeners felt the warmth of Bodett's voice and imagined he was talking directly to them.

John Updike used to say that he liked to imagine some young kid in a Midwestern town finding his book in the local library. Novelist Padgett Powell writes for a girl who rejected his love ten years ago, hoping to make her realize what a mistake she made. Gabriel García Márquez writes for his friends.

Think about the need you are hoping to fill, the person you wish to touch with your work. Put someone's picture over your desk, or keep your ideal reader in mind.

variations

According to William Gass, "Getting even is one of the great reasons for writing." NPR commentator, poet, and novelist Andrei Codrescu says he writes to wreak revenge on the people who tormented him when he was growing up. "When you're a child the adults fuck you over and you try to imagine some way to get back at them. One way is to become a famous writer." Writing is a terrific way to get back at people, he says, "because you can absolutely savage them and that will be their portrait for eternity. It's better than killing them. Killing, you just get rid of the body. This way you can torture the spirit."

Dedicate your talent to righting a wrong. Israeli author Amos Oz often writes because he's filled with rage. "I feel I have to tell my government what to do and where to go." If you are angry about something, vent. Lots of people may share your grievance, and your words can give them courage and ammunition with which to fight for change.

Write about someone who made your life miserable. Do an exposé. Cast this person as a pitiful villain. Give her some hideous deformity. Exaggerate his weaknesses. Make him suffer.

Looking for a way to begin this chapter, I reached for the *Collins Dictionary of Literary Quotations* sitting above my desk. There I found these words from Oliver Wendell Holmes: "When I feel inclined to read poetry, I take down my dictionary. The poetry of words is quite as beautiful as that of sentences. The author may arrange the gems effectively, but their shape and luster have been given by the attrition of ages."

Pulitzer Prize–winning novelist Carol Shields, author of *The Stone Diaries*, often

visit a

Dictionary

begins her writing day by reading from the dictionary. She picks a page at random and spends the next five minutes reading every word. Shields does this not to find a word to use but to immerse herself in language. It centers her, and slows her down so that she can write.

As a young journalist, Sophy Burnham, author of the best-selling *Book of Angels*, as well as *Revelations* and *For Writers Only*, used to play a game when faced with a boring assignment. She would search the dictionary for "an obscure and magnificent word" and then challenge herself to incorporate it into the text. She once constructed an entire chapter around the unpronounceable word *autochthons,* even though it was unrelated to her subject.

Let a dictionary serve as a stimulator for you today. Pick a word at random—or scan until one word catches your eye—and use it in a sentence. Let the sentence lead you to a paragraph and from there to a page. This method of writing may seem nonsensical at first, but within minutes you will find yourself coming up with ideas that feed directly into your work. If you don't have a project you are currently working on, this spontaneous writing can easily guide you into an area worth exploring. As Freud discovered a century ago, a word or image can quickly lead to the fundamental issues occupying your unconscious mind.

To help myself loosen up in the morning, I have a deck of index cards on which I've inscribed simple nouns and verbs. I often begin my writing day by pulling one from the pile and expanding on that word for about ten minutes, writing anything and everything it evokes in my mind. *The Observation Deck* chapter called "Dedicate" evolved from an improvisation on the word *mouth,* which brought to mind the Jewish prayer I say to myself before giving a speech: "May the words of my mouth and the meditation of my heart be acceptable to you, O Lord. . . ." I realized how much easier it is for me to create when I focus on serving others rather than on impressing people with my wit.

Third World development specialist Michael Mercil uses the dictionary to help Peace Corps volunteers get to know each other while discovering their own natural creativity. Each person is assigned three unrelated words out of which he must make an impromptu, three-minute speech. The connections people make are extraordinary. You might try this game with several friends and see what happens. Or take three minutes to improvise alone on a piece of paper.

Jacquelyn Mitchard, author of the best-selling novel *Deep End of the Ocean*, likes to make lists of odd words which she can incorporate into her writing in unusual ways. She didn't know what *celibacy* had to do with her story, but as soon as she put the word into a sentence she saw her heroine's numbness as a choice to forsake all emotion, thus a celibacy of the heart.

You can gain new insight into any subject by learning the etymology of the words that describe it. I was fascinated to learn that the word *sarcophagus,* which is a type of stone coffin, derives from the Greek *sarkophagos*, which means flesh-eating stone. Suddenly I realized that these beautiful stone coffins once contained rotting bodies. Death was no longer an abstraction, but a foul-smelling reality.

You can also find inspiration in other reference books. Best-selling children's book author Jack Prelutsky *(New Kid on the Block)* once had a thesaurus practically write a poem for him. When he was writing about a very large dinosaur, he looked up the word *huge.* The thesaurus featured seven synonyms, arranged in such an order that, if he put a line in front of each, the first and fourth lines would rhyme. Realizing that if he could find a word to rhyme with the sixth he'd have a poem, he wrote:

Seismosaurus was enormous

Seismosaurus was tremendous

Seismosaurus was prodigious

Seismosaurus was stupendous

Seismosaurus was titanic

Seismosaurus was colossal

Seismosaurus now is nothing

But a monumental fossil

Take a look at your bookshelves and find another reference book to use for inspiration. Pick a page at random from an atlas and write a poem about that place. Open an encyclopedia and write a love song mentioning the first topic on the left-hand page. Pull a name from the phone book and write a description of that person's living room. None of this has to be for publication, it is simply a way to get loosened up and have a little fun.

"Originality is nothing but judicious imitation," wrote Voltaire. "The most original writers borrowed from one another." And in so doing, they developed their own craft.

Many of us suffer from the crippling notion that we must reinvent the techniques of storytelling. But in art, as in science, we build on the work of those who have gone before. Sir Isaac Newton said, "If I have seen far, it is because I have stood on the shoulders of giants."

Masters

As a young writer, Joan Didion typed out Hemingway stories to "learn how his sentences worked." Francine Du Plessix Gray filled notebooks with paragraphs copied from T. S. Eliot and Henry James. And, for a time, Somerset Maugham transcribed one page of Jonathan Swift each day.

The act of physically transcribing helped these writers imprint the rhythms and structures of effective language onto their brains. They were teaching their hands what it felt like to create the kind of sentences they admired.

If you are having trouble with some aspect of your work today—whether it's dialogue, rhythm, mood, place, character, or structure—pull out a few of your favorite books and see how other authors have solved the same problem. Try writing a conversation or a description in the manner of an author you admire. You might write it several times in the styles of several different authors. You can even rewrite it in the manner of someone whose work you despise, just to get your juices flowing.

If you are interested in learning to write dialogue, novelist Clyde Edgerton suggests you read Hemingway's "Hills Like White Elephants"—a story in which the crisis facing a couple is exposed entirely through dialogue—and then write a piece in Hemingway's style. If you prefer, try to emulate the language and rhythms of a Tennessee Williams drama. Or see if you can produce the kind of rapid repartee Elmore Leonard creates in his novels.

If you wish to write more like one particular author, read a page of his or her work out loud to discover what specific things make it so effective. Find something specific that you can emulate, then play around with the technique. I didn't know why I liked Anne Lamott so much until I read her writing aloud for this exercise and realized the wonderful wackiness of her metaphors. I would never think to describe dialogue as "so purple that it reads like something from a childhood play by the Gabor sisters," but reading this I realized I could have more fun with analogies, and set about to come up with a list of ten.

If you consciously emulate another person's style, you will not end up with a cheap imitation. After experimenting a while with another writer's technique, you will invariably make it your own. You will carry it further, delve deeper, and change the style to fit your own message.

If you are worried about seeming derivative, novelist Clyde Edgerton says, "Just relax. You are attracted to another writer's work because you share certain sensibilities." It is natural that you will gravitate to similar forms of expression. But your unique history and way of seeing the world guarantee that your work will have a style all its own.

Woody Allen's earliest writing was actually an imitation of Max Shulman and S. J. Perelman. After several of his pieces were accepted by the *New Yorker*, the editors warned Allen that he risked appearing dangerously derivative, so from then on he consciously worked to simplify his writing and find his own voice. But Allen never stopped learning from other artists. In an interview for *The Art of Humor,* he remarked, "The biggest influences on me, I guess, have been Bergman and the Marx Brothers. I also have no compunction stealing from Strindberg, Chekhov, Perelman, Moss Hart, Jimmy Cannon, Fellini, and Bob Hope's writers."

It is important to emphasize here that I am not suggesting plagiarism. You do not take someone else's words and pretend they're your own. Nor do you change a word or two and try to pass off a sentence as original.

"The instruction we find in books is like fire," wrote Voltaire. "We fetch it from our neighbors, kindle it at home, communicate it to others, and it becomes the property of all."

Do not limit yourself to reading your own genre. Fiction writers can benefit from reading nonfiction, and nonfiction writers can gain a lot from novels. For his true accounts of scientific discovery, Wade Davis employs various literary techniques. When he wants to describe a landscape he may read a bit of T. E. Lawrence first. Before embarking on a character description, he might read some Lawrence Durrell.

My sister Julia often reads a bit of Isabel Allende or Gabriel García Márquez when she is working on a grant proposal to raise money for a nonprofit group. She almost always gets her projects funded, in part because she strives to evoke images of the human beings that the project would benefit. If she is trying to raise money for a new ambulance system, she might make the funders imagine a woman lying bloody in the street, being revived by a paramedic. She can show them the fear in a loved one's eyes, waiting for an ambulance to appear. And in so doing, she can make her funders feel like heroes when they come up with the money.

Writer Julie Winokur suggests that you play with the idea that one of your characters is trying to imitate someone else, real or fictional. You might create a character who perceives himself as James Bond or David Bowie. How does this impact his style of speech, his physical appearance, his thoughts and actions?

Write a parody of a book, film, song, or TV commercial. Aldous Huxley said that *Brave New World* began as a parody of "Men Like Gods" by H. G. Wells, but it gradually "got out of hand and became something quite different." You might write a dishwashing aria in the style of Verdi or describe a children's birthday party as if you were Danielle Steele. Adapting an incongruous voice to a mundane subject will help you find humor or drama you might otherwise have missed.

set realistic

Goals

S cott Adams was a thirty-year-old middle manager working in a windowless cubicle and dreaming of becoming a famous cartoonist, when he realized that he might never accomplish anything unless he set some realistic goals. Not wanting to set his expectations too high, he told himself that he must simply get one cartoon published somewhere, anywhere, before he died. With that in mind, he began preparing a packet of strips caricaturing corporate life and mailed them out.

Nine years later, Adams's cartoon strip *Dilbert* is being published in more than 1,000 newspapers in thirty-two countries. Two of his books were on the *New York Times* best-seller list simultaneously—*The Dilbert Principle* and *Dogbert's Top Secret Management Handbook*.

"Most people set goals ineffectively," says Dr. Neil Fiore, author of *The Now Habit* and *Overcoming Procrastination*. Rather than setting concrete, achievable goals, they tell themselves that they must do the impossible. They think, "I have to write a best-selling novel," instead of "I will make a list of potential characters for a story right now." It's "I must find an agent," rather than, "For the next ten or twenty minutes, I will brainstorm ten chapter titles."

You have to create attainable goals, things you can begin to accomplish right away, yet you also need a larger vision to sustain you. Take a few minutes to imagine where you'd like to be ten years from now. Choose one specific thing you'd like to accomplish as a writer in that time. Now work backwards from the future. Draw a time line from then to now and fill in the milestones you must pass along the way. Choose one action to take today. If you want to become the world's leading writer on mushroom hunting, concentrate on getting a short article written for the mycological society newsletter. Or write a letter to your local paper announcing a mushroom hunt.

Focus on what you can actually do in the next few hours. Make the activity simple—create an outline, sketch out a character, identify a conflict—then sit down and do it.

To keep your larger dream in mind, Scott Adams suggests you formulate an affirmation and write it down frequently. When he was preparing the first *Dilbert* strips, he wrote the words *I will become a syndicated columnist* fifteen times a day, every day, until the comic strip was picked up by United Media. Adams does not know why affirmations work, but he has seen them make a difference in his life and the lives of many others. "Besides," he says, "there are no harmful side effects and they do help focus your energy."

Feel free to modify a goal if it seems too difficult or becomes too easy. Start with something you know you can do—even though it may be a stretch. I find it a challenge to turn the phone off for fifteen minutes but, knowing that this is essential if I'm to get any work done, I trust in voice mail and create short-term, phone-free writing goals.

Some writers tell themselves they must put in a certain number of hours each day; others challenge themselves to write a specific number of words. For ten years, Ray Bradbury set a goal of one thousand words per day and one story per week. On Monday he wrote a first draft, on Tuesday a second draft, and on Saturday he mailed the sixth draft to New York. Sundays he was free to think up new ideas.

Graham Greene had a different method. He wrote exactly five hundred words a day. As soon as he reached that magic number he stopped, no matter what time it was or where he was in a story.

Kurt Vonnegut set different goals for every project. When he began *Cat's Cradle*, he told himself that he need only create one chapter per day, no matter what the length. As a consequence, the book contains one chapter, entitled "What God Is," that is just eleven lines (seventy-seven words) long.

Mary Pipher, author of *Reviving Ophelia*, says that she's too busy to commit to any sort of daily routine so she sets herself monthly goals, which she breaks down into manageable daily chunks. Looking at what she needs to accomplish and what she can accomplish, she might determine that she needs to spend ten hours on a project that week. She can then work two hours a day for five days or work all ten hours in one day, as long as she meets her projected quota.

Pipher recommends that you keep a record of how many hours you work each day and how many hours each week. Give yourself credit for whatever you do and, she says, "Recognize that not all work consists of writing and not all writing results in useable output."

Experiment to find a method and a standard that works for you. You may discover you write best late at night or early in the morning. You may find that you prefer time limits, word counts, or small, discreet tasks. Right now, set an easy writing goal and then do it. You can always try a different goal tomorrow. If you were unable to meet today's goal, create a more realistic one for tomorrow.

"If one advances confidently in the direction of his dreams, and endeavors to live the life which he has imagined," Henry David Thoreau wrote, "he will meet with a success unexpected in common hours."

If you are working on fiction, biography, or memoir, examine the goals of one of your characters. Ask yourself if these are realistic goals. What are the things getting in your character's way? What are the goals that other people are trying to impose on your character? Write these things down and then go back to your story.

If you are writing nonfiction, ask yourself what you want the piece to accomplish. Do you want to entertain? To enrage? To elicit action? If your goals have been nebulous, make them concrete. If they have been unrealistic, modify them.

variations

Tim Parks had already written 350 pages of the novel *Goodness* when he found himself losing interest in his characters' marital woes. He decided he had to raise the stakes—make the couple's problems become a matter of life or death—so he gave them a brain-damaged child. Suddenly the writing took off. Parks realized that most of what he'd written up to that point could be eliminated. He dropped the first 250 pages of the novel and it became a much better book.

raise the

Stakes

How can you raise the stakes in your story? Is the conflict between characters too tame? Have you shown your nonfiction readers what they have to lose if they don't accept your argument?

If you are trying to convince people not to destroy the rain forest, don't just talk about the loss of pretty flowers; show how millions of people will die without the oxygen those trees provide. Make your readers gasp for air as you paint a picture of the world in twenty years.

Ken Follett says that you need the stakes to be high for every one of your fictional characters. If you are writing about a bank robbery, make sure that your robber has a compelling need to steal the money. It's not enough that he wants to be rich. He needs to have an ambitious plan that requires a million dollars. He has to have someone or something that will die without the money. The bank should also be at serious risk if a million dollars is lost. Maybe the bank's insurance has been canceled or the banker is in serious debt, having "borrowed" funds to cover a secret gambling loss.

Novelist Georges Simenon began to work on each of his books by placing two characters in a location and asking himself, "What can happen to them that will cause them to reach their limit?" He would then focus on a simple incident that would radically change these people's lives.

Imagine a situation that would push a character or a set of characters to the limits of their endurance. This might be a physical challenge—like climbing a mountain in a snowstorm—or it might be the loss of an only child. Make a list, then pick one situation and push it even further. Make the loss of a child the result of rape and murder. By a family friend. In the family home. Increase the challenge of a ski race by having your hero's family watching when a snowstorm hits. Make the hero's rival someone who has brought great shame to the family, someone who will profit by your hero's loss. Whatever troubles you're describing, make them bad and then make them even worse.

Examine the realm that lies beneath the surface—the world that is usually unseen. Discover the dark side of your hero, the soft side of your villain. Explore the side effects of the cure you're advocating. Determine who may suffer in allowing someone to win a war.

Every positive characteristic has its negative side. The generous woman may have a hard time saying no. The frugal saver may be unable to buy things that he needs. The diligent worker may be incapable of

explore the
Underside

acting spontaneously, the free spirit incapable of getting down to work.

Children's book author and poet Judith Viorst says that when amateur stories for kids don't work, it is often because the writers make their heroes too good. Children do not like stories in which another child is perfect. They need to see that they are not the only ones who are jealous of a sibling or resent the need to share. Charlotte, the spider in *Charlotte's Web,* has a bloodthirsty aspect. In *Harriet the Spy,* Harriet writes cruel things about her friends.

Readers enjoy Hannibal Lector in *The*

Silence of the Lambs because he is clever, witty, and takes pleasure in his work. People delight in Captain Hook because he is vain and afraid of a crocodile.

Write a scene that reveals an unexpected aspect of a character. Show the goodness of your bad guy, the badness of the one who seems so good. If you are writing about an institution, make sure you know its underside (even if you choose not to show it). Try to understand the needs of the oppressor as well as those of the victim when describing inequality or abuse.

Take a look at the actual underside of an object. Pick up a rock and see what lies beneath it. Notice the worms and sowbugs thriving in the dark. Look under a piece of furniture and see what its owner is trying to hide. Take a piece of machinery apart—a watch, a toaster, a broken toy—to see how it really works. By focusing your attention on the details that reside below the surface, you are training yourself to write with greater depth.

Look for the action behind the scenes, the unnamed people who make a company function, the puppeteer who pulls the strings, the lighting technician who brings the stage to life.

Find what is hidden in a closet—the closet of a character or the closet you've neglected in your home. You may find forgotten treasures or powerful skeletons to expose.

Gabriel García Márquez was browsing in a Roman bookstore when he came upon a photograph that crystallized the vague image that had been floating in his mind. This picture, of cows grazing on the curtains of a luxurious palace, inspired him to begin *The Autumn of the Patriarch*.

"You get the best ideas in the whole world looking at old photograph books," says Newbery Award–winning author Patricia MacLachlan. "They're the most amazing jumping-off points. They have a

study a
Photograph

reverberation from then to here." For years, MacLachlan has found inspiration staring at old WPA photographs from the Depression era, imagining the joys and tragedies of the people she sees portrayed.

Pulitzer Prize–winning author Carol Shields sometimes brings photos into her creative writing classes. She asks the students to list everything they can about the person in a picture. Then she'll ask a series of questions, such as: Does this person believe in God? Who might his or her best friend be? Does this person like Shakespeare?

Make a list of questions you might ask

about an unknown person in a photograph. What kind of vehicle would he drive? Where would she keep her money? What would he have eaten for breakfast? Who are the people she loves? Find a photo in a book or magazine and ask yourself these questions and more. Create a history or verbal portrait. When writing a story, you may only reveal a fraction of what you've learned, but knowing so much about your characters will help you fully develop them.

As a young boy growing up in the backwoods of Georgia, writer Harry Crews used to make up stories about the models in the Sears and Roebuck catalog. "I knew that under those fancy clothes there had to be swellings and boils of one kind or another," he wrote in his memoir, *A Childhood*. Crews sometimes put people from different pages together in unusual situations and let dramas develop. See what happens when you create a scene with two or more photographic subjects.

"What should I do without this family cemetery which makes everything so perfectly clear?" asks Oskar, the mad hero of Gunter Grass's *The Tin Drum*, referring to his photo album. While studying pictures of his mother, father, and Uncle Jan, Oskar comes to understand the triad that governed his childhood. He finds clues to a secret love affair in the placement of a hand upon a shoulder, the props that appear in a formal pose, and the absence of a certain face from the family album.

Pull out your own photo collection. Let one picture catch your eye or allow a succession of images provide insight into someone's development or decline. Let these images inspire you to write—about the time, incidents, or emotions the photographs evoke.

Thomas Keneally, author of *Schindler's List*, found a pair of family photos, each depicting one of the two general stores his grandparents had owned in the dusty town of Kempsy, Australia. One bore a sign with his grandfather's initials, while the other bore the initials of his grandmother. Keneally began writing *A River Town*, his twenty-first novel, to explore what caused the change.

Perhaps a question will arise for you while looking at old family photos, as it did for me on discovering a photo of my grandmother in her twenties. I had no idea that the old woman who hid in an upstairs bedroom mending our clothes had ever laughed. Or that she had once been beautiful. Seeing this picture led me to ask others about my grandmother's life and to uncover the tragedies that had transformed her.

You may notice a pattern in the photos you have saved. My album is full of old boyfriends and dogs. What images have you chosen to keep? Notice the changes wrought by age and fashion. What do these photos say about the people who snapped the shutters? What do they say about the times when they were taken? Pay attention to what is not in a picture as well as what sits in the periphery.

If you are currently writing about another time or place, you will find old picture books a valuable resource. Examine the hairstyles, the clothing, the props. (If the time you are describing is one that precedes the camera's invention, study paintings of that era.) It would be difficult to imagine E. L. Doctorow writing *Waterworks*, Jack Finney writing *Time and Again*, or Caleb Carr writing *The Alienist* without consulting photographs of old New York.

In 1862, Henry David Thoreau wrote, "I think that I cannot preserve my health and spirits, unless I spend four hours a day at least . . . sauntering through the woods and over the hills and fields, absolutely free from all earthly engagements."

I doubt you can afford four hours a day for wandering about, but even if you walk for just twenty minutes today it will give new energy to your work. As you walk, you can think about a current project, make up stories about things you pass, or simply

Take a Walk

allow your thoughts to wander. No matter where you focus your attention, part of you is working below the surface, solving problems, generating ideas.

Carlos Fuentes used to compose in his head as he walked so that, upon reaching his desk, he'd have five or six pages to transcribe onto paper.

Richard Paul Evans, whose first novel, *The Christmas Box*, sold over two million copies, credits a walk with helping him break through writer's block. On a long hike through the woods he realized that the heroine of his second novel, *The Time Piece*, could not die of scarlet fever as he had planned, but must perish in a fire. This revelation solved several technical problems and put the story back in motion.

Thornton Wilder, William Saroyan, Thomas Wolfe, and Ray Bradbury have each spoken of the importance of walking in their lives. Wilder called his morning ritual a springboard to help him begin writing each day. Saroyan used the time he spent walking to and from his studio to "observe the human condition reflected in the faces he passed." Bradbury and Wolfe both found inspiration wandering city streets at night, alone.

Allow yourself the pleasure of a walk today. Is there an errand you could do on foot? A park where you can wander? A neighborhood to explore? Carry a notebook or some three-by-five index cards to capture any new thoughts, or let them percolate and then write when you get home. If walking is a daily habit, take a different route or move at a different speed. Write about what you see, feel, think, and remember.

If it's nighttime and you don't feel safe outside, take a walk around the inside of your house or apartment building. Walk slowly, touching things, running your hand over furniture. Lift various objects and feel their shape and texture. Explore your home as if you were seeing it for the first time. Then, sit down and see what emerges on paper. You may or may not write about the experience itself. The act of moving around and exploring can alter your consciousness enough that you return to your desk stimulated and refreshed.

Walking is a wonderful way to become centered, focused, and calm. In *Wherever You Go, There You Are*, Jon Kabat Zinn describes the Zen practice known as walking meditation. Rather than focusing on the external world or worrying about your past, present, or future, you simply pay attention to the internal sensations you experience as you move through space. Notice the feeling in the soles of your feet as they touch the ground and then lift off. Listen to the sound of each footstep. Focus on the movement of

your breath.

While walking, I find that narrowing or even closing my eyes to eliminate visual stimuli helps me achieve a state of peace which makes writing easier. You needn't travel far to do a walking meditation. You can walk in circles or up and down a narrow path. When working on speeches, I used to walk round and round a park near my house, speaking my lines out loud.

Walking does not have to be a solitary activity. Many great thinkers work out their ideas while walking the streets with friends. Who knows who you might meet? Ernest Hemingway met Gertrude Stein walking in the Tuileries in Paris.

To give your walk focus, look for an object that might symbolize a particular idea or emotion. I recently gave myself the task of finding something to represent darkness and light. After twenty minutes, I came upon a group of luminescent white mushrooms poking up through the rich brown dirt. Continuing on, I began to notice the light reflected in drops of water and spider webs hanging in the trees.

Take a walk as if you were one of your characters. Play with your posture, your speed, and the locus of your attention. Notice the things your character would see. A criminal might keep his eyes open for unlocked doors and passing patrol cars; an expectant mother, for strollers and crying children.

If you feel you need to stay at your desk, take an imaginary walk through one of your character's neighborhoods. Envision people you'd pass, see the buildings and trees. Imagine the smell of the air, the feel of the sidewalk, the sounds of the street. In your mind, stroll through your character's home or office and examine the objects you find.

When you walk, don't let old baggage drag you down. Travel light and learn from the people and things you meet on your journey.

When, as a kid, I found myself unable to start or finish homework, my father would say, *"Ribe tuchus!"* Translated from the Yiddish, this means "rub your bottom on the chair." Sometimes this is exactly what you have to do. Sit, even if you don't think you have anything to write. Sit until the muse says, "Okay, I guess you're serious. Maybe I'll drop in and dispense a little inspiration." If you're always running around, she may never find you. So put your seat on that chair.

Ribe Tuchus

Flannery O'Connor used to force herself to sit for three hours every day. If she couldn't write she would simply stare at the wall.

In an essay called "And Zen I Wrote," NPR commentator and children's author Daniel Pinkwater explained how he created a regimen to overcome his trouble getting started. He made himself sit at a table for one hour every day. He didn't have to write, but he was not allowed to do anything else. The mere act of sitting still for an hour was regarded as a successful day's work. Pinkwater gradually increased the time and discovered that if he could sit still for two hours, he'd eventually start writing just to pass the time. After a while the writing improved.

This deck has a lot of cards that encourage you to go ahead, get out of your chair, do this or that. But today is your day to sit still and see what happens. Set a timer for one hour and sit. You do not have to write, but I wouldn't be surprised if, somewhere in the next sixty minutes, you find the urge to write greater than any resistance you might have had. The writing does not have to be good. It can be lousy. But repeat this card for a week; *ribe tuchus* for an hour a day and see what develops.

This card does not have many variations. Your job is to simply sit at your writing table. If you need something to write about, pull another card and let the phrase on the card provide a jumping-off place for your writing.

No, you may not leave the table. Stay put. Write about anything or nothing at all. Write about resistance. Write about chairs. Whatever you do, keep your bottom on the seat until the hour is up.

variations

M y sister Julia called recently, wanting to know what she could do to be more creative in her writing. Her office felt cold and sterile and she was having a hard time getting to work. She'd just seen *Frank and Ollie,* a documentary about two Disney animators, and had been struck by the cozy clutter with which these men surrounded themselves. Julia thought that maybe the atmosphere in their studios contributed to the quality of their work.

We both pictured what made each man's

create a

Sacred Space

office so alive: all sorts of images pinned to the walls, pictures from magazines, drawings from friends. As we talked, she began gathering favorite things from around the house—a perfume bottle shaped like a heart, a mezuzah her twin had given her, some plants, a set of candlesticks, a branch from a eucalyptus tree. She arranged these objects on top of a filing cabinet, creating an altar of things she loved. After we hung up, she brought more things into the room. When she finally sat down to write, the words flowed. She called three days later to say that, for the first time in her life, she couldn't wait to get back to her office to write; her work was going wonderfully.

This corner of her office became a sacred space, a place to focus spiritual and creative energies so that they could be expressed through her work.

Make your workspace into an altar, a sacred place where ideas and archetypes can act out their dramas. Put pictures of loved ones on your desk. Place a flower in a vase or an object of beauty in your sight line.

Perhaps you have the opposite problem from Julia's—your workspace is too cluttered. I am constantly having to move my literary escort business off the desk so I can write without distraction. Bills and invoices have to be out of sight in order for me to work.

Of course, you may not even have a desk to work at. The kitchen table or a library carrel might be where you go to write. Still, you need a special place to keep your writing materials—a box, drawer, or briefcase. When you get your writing tools out to work, recognize that you are entering a special state of mind. Take time to arrange everything. Treat this preparation as a ritual which helps focus your energy on the project at hand.

Interviewing Isabel Allende for *Writers Dreaming*, I was struck by her air of grace and asked if she had a secret that allowed her such serenity. "Fresh flowers" was her surprising reply. She has always kept fresh flowers around her. Even when she could not afford to buy them, she would pick them from a neighbor's field.

It may not be possible to find fresh flowers midwinter in Minnesota, but a sprig of evergreen will make a room smell wonderful. Some oranges or a pile of apples will add color and fragrance to your space.

If you want to invoke a spirit of playfulness, surround yourself with toys or cartoons. Children's poet Jack Prelutsky works in an office filled with plastic frogs and wind-up creatures.

If you are writing about a far off-land, surround yourself with images of that place and its people. Patricia MacLachlan carries a bag full of prairie dust wherever she goes to remind her of the world in which her characters live.

Your desk need not be neat—it need not be a desk at all—but make it a sacred spot that will entice your muse to visit.

You may want to dedicate your workspace to people or things that you love and admire. Mystery writer Julie Smith has created a shrine to her favorite writers just above her desk. At the center on a velvet cloth, sits Julie's Edgar Award—a bust of Edgar Alan Poe—which she has crowned with a tiara and festooned with Mardi Gras beads. To the left and right she has hung pictures of Tennessee Williams and William Faulkner. At the top is a photo of Eudora Welty. With "Tom, Bill, Ed, and Miss Welty" around her, she feels much less alone.

"**S**pecificity is generosity," says National Book Award–winning novelist Charles Johnson, author of *The Middle Passage*. "The more detail you give your readers, the more you help their imaginations."

In an interview with the *Paris Review*, Gabriel García Márquez showed how he used specificity to make even the most fantastical events ring true. "If you say that there are elephants flying in the sky, people are not going to believe you. But if you say that there are four hundred and twenty-five

Get Specific

elephants in the sky, people probably will believe you."

Marquez, author of *One Hundred Years of Solitude*, learned the magic of specificity from a grandmother who used to say that every time the electrician came around, the house was filled with yellow butterflies. When trying to use this image in one of his stories, Marquez discovered that if he did not say the butterflies were yellow, people would not believe him.

Critiquing a script by Caroline Marshall, screenwriter Terry Southern (*The Magic Christian, Candy, Dr. Strangelove*) crossed out the words *red dress,* exclaiming, "Never just say red dress. Be specific: ultra revealing micro mini with fringe."

Novelist W. E. Reinka suggests comparing "The child sat under the tree, eating a piece of fruit" with "Johnny sat under the maple, eating a banana." He says, "Clearly it is easier to picture a banana than it is to envision a generic fruit."

Take a look at something you have written and circle any passages that might be vague. If you've been discussing an abstract idea, give a concrete example or illustrate it with an anecdote. Replace general nouns and adjectives with words that are more specific. You want your readers to see the same things that you see. If you've said that your character drives a sports car, say what kind of sports car. Don't let readers imagine him in a green MG Midget or a yellow Miata when he wouldn't be caught dead in anything but a black Lamborghini.

Show, don't tell!—a cardinal rule of writing—is another way of saying "be specific." Don't tell us the man got angry; show him punching a hole through the motel wall or biting through his lower lip. Don't tell us the war was brutal, do as Richard Price suggests: show us the burnt socks of children lying by the side of the road.

Adam Robinson suggests a simple exercise. Take an adjective you've recently employed and drop it into this sentence: He was so [insert adjective] that he once _____. If you find yourself saying a character was reckless, show just how reckless he was. He was so reckless that he once _____. Or, if the day was cold, it was so cold that _____.

In interviews, encourage your subjects to clarify abstract terms and give concrete examples. In *Writers Dreaming,* I always followed up my questions with phrases such as "What do you mean?" "Could you give me an example?" "Please explain." The initial reply to my inquiries was usually vague or superficial. But by pushing each author to be specific, I was able to elicit detailed accounts of the creative process and to learn techniques that would otherwise have been glossed over.

If you are writing an essay, Stephen Jay Gould suggests you examine something small and make larger points about it. To talk about evolution, Gould examined the development of the panda's thumb.

As Goethe once said, "The poet should seize the particular; and he should, if there be anything in it, thus represent the universal."

"The cat sat on the mat and that was that"—this is the kind of rhyme that Maya Angelou writes when she is feeling stuck. Anything to keep the pen moving. Anything to let the muse know that she is present at her desk and ready for a visit.

Everybody knows how to rhyme. June rhymes with spoon and moon. So what if it's been done before? Have some fun with rhyming, if only to loosen the goose and let the juice start flowing.

Rhyme

Take a few minutes to play with rhyme. Pick a word, any word. Preferably a short one.

> Short one.
> Top gun.
> Who won?
> Father? son?
> Gotta run.
> Is this done?
> I hope so!

Take a headline from the newspaper. Let the last syllable be your guide:

Edmund Muskie Dies.
He had pouchy eyes,
Not too many guys
that tries
to be president
succeed.
Indeed!
I feel a need
to take the lead
and rhyme all day.
No way José.
That's how we play.

Clearly this is not about making art. It is about freeing up your playful side and seeing what comes out. Sure, a lot of the rhymes may prove childish or sexual—but what a nice way to while away a few minutes and uncover rich material.

Much of Arthur Miller's *Death of a Salesman* and all of *The Crucible* were originally written in verse. Miller converted his plays into prose because "as soon as an American actor sees something printed like verse, he immediately puts one foot in front of the other—or else he mutters. Then you can't hear it at all."

As Oliver Wendell Holmes said, "When you write in prose you say what you mean. When you write in rhyme you say what you must."

Playwright Robert Anderson was having trouble writing when he called John Steinbeck asking for help. Steinbeck said: "I told him to write poetry—not for selling, not even for seeing—poetry to throw away. For poetry is the mathematics of writing and closely akin to music. And it is also the best therapy because sometimes the troubles come tumbling out."

"I rhyme to see myself, to set the darkness echoing," said poet Seamus Heaney. "I rhyme for fun," wrote Robert Burns.

Point of View

Sue Grafton knew that her first book, *A Is for Alibi*, had to be followed by one called *B Is for Burglar*, but the second story was not coming together. She considered changing the title to B Is for Blackmail or B Is for Burning but, as she said in *Writers Dreaming*, "I have a certain interior writing machine that's very stubborn and dominating, and this little machine said, 'No ma'am, I'm sorry but this book is called *B is for Burglar.*'" So she put the book aside until one night an internal voice roused her

from sleep. "I suddenly understood I was to take the same story and tell it from a different angle. So, where I had originally opened the book with the burglar's point of view I simply shifted off to another character. I could retain all the work I had done but just give it a different form."

Gloria Naylor, author of the National Book Award–winning novel *The Women of Brewster Place*, was suffering from acute writer's block when she picked up a copy of William Faulkner's *As I Lay Dying*. Suddenly she saw the nature of her problem. Naylor had been trying to write *Mama Day* in the third person and in past tense— a style that had worked well in her first two books. But this story, like Faulkner's, needed to be told by a series of different characters. "I didn't know anything about writing in the first person and I was terrified. But that was neither here nor there. That was what had to happen."

Anytime you feel stuck, try telling your story from another point of view. Even if your final piece ends up being told by the original narrator, you will gain surprising insights from this simple exercise. If you are writing a story from the point of view of an unhappy boy, describe an incident in the voice of his beleaguered mother. If you are using an omniscient narrator to relate a bit of history, describe an event through the eyes of one or more participants.

Retell a fairy tale from the point of view of the ogre, witch, or simpleton. Take Rumpelstiltskin's side of the story. He fulfilled his part of the bargain by spinning the straw into gold. Clearly the queen was wrong to renege on her promise!

Don't limit yourself. If you are writing about the way a certain virus works, describe the human body through a virus's "eyes." Or from the viewpoint of a cell about to be invaded.

Show us a moment in military history through the eyes of the women left behind. Describe the war as it might have been experienced by a vanquished general, a weary camp follower, a galley slave.

Take on the voice of an inanimate object and view the world through its eyes. For *The Floatplane Notebooks*, Clyde Edgerton wanted a narrator who had witnessed one family's life through several generations. He chose a wisteria vine to fill that role, opening with the words *I was planted by the back door steps the day Thomas Pittman died.*

You might want to adapt the technique that gestalt psychologist Fritz Perls developed for the interpretation of dreams. Assume that every element in a dream, a nightmare, or even a story represents a part of you. Let some element speak. Find out what the old house has to tell you about yourself, hear the concerns that the rusty sewing machine manifests. Think about the message of the clock sitting on your desk.

Pretend you are an object—a cup, a shoe, a book, or a pen. Write about this object in the first person. Give it a voice. Using the words "I am . . ." describe your size, shape, color, texture, and how you feel in your surroundings. You can develop your monologue into a story, essay, or poem—or simply enjoy the insights you gain.

In her seminal book *Dream Power,* Ann Faraday relates how a woman discovered the underlying resentment she felt toward her family when she spoke in the voice of a stove that had blown up in her dream: "I sit here in the kitchen and people ignore me; if someone doesn't pay attention to me soon I'm going to explode."

feed your

Senses

"I learn as much from painters about how to write as from writers," said Ernest Hemingway, who spent countless afternoons absorbing the art of the impressionists in the Musée du Luxembourg. When asked by the *Paris Review* to name his literary forebears, Hemingway listed not only writers but Brueghel, Cézanne, van Gogh, Gauguin, Hieronymus Bosch, and Mozart. Studying the work of these artists was, for Hemingway, "part of learning to see, to hear, to feel and not feel, and to write."

Poet Allen Ginsberg used to spend hours in the basement of New York's Museum of Modern Art studying the watercolors. "That's where I began turning on to space in Cézanne and the way he built it up," he said. Ginsberg paid homage to Cézanne in the poem *Howl*, juxtaposing words as the painter had juxtaposed colors.

When Newbery Award–winning author Patricia MacLachlan is feeling stuck, she will take a break and attend a concert or visit a museum, searching for just one piece that will move her. "This renews me and brings me back to what we're doing as artists—that is, saying something fresh and taking risks."

As a writer, you need—and deserve—sensual, sensory adventure. Find an exhibit, a concert, or a performance to attend. If today doesn't work, find a day that will, and reserve it on your calendar. Take a long lunch hour or leave work early to explore someplace special. Arrange for someone to relieve you for a few hours and enjoy an extended outing.

You need not restrict your adventure to an art museum or symphony concert. The most wonderful creations are the works of mother nature and of ordinary people. Go where you can see, hear, smell, feel, or taste something that has been made with care, joy, or deliberation. Visit a place of natural beauty and enjoy a sense of peace and wonder. Go to a site of historical interest and let your imagination travel back in time.

Perhaps there is an exhibit nearby—of musical instruments, Indian textiles, or cowboy paraphernalia—that you can visit. It might be housed in a corporate lobby, a gallery, or a shopping mall. Look in the paper and see what is going on in your area. There may be a demonstration of tribal dances, martial arts, or puppeteering you'd otherwise have missed.

Even if you live in a very small town, you can find people who turn the ordinary into art. This may be your local florist or a shopkeeper who creates unusual window displays. It may be a neighbor who does quilting on the side. Seek out this person's work. Visit their shop, studio, or bakery and learn what makes this work appealing. Or spend an hour in the library and examine some illustrated books.

When attending a show or concert, I love to imagine myself inside the mind of the creator. Sometimes I ask myself, "What was this artist trying to accomplish? How did he or she alter the tradition? What kind of stages must he or she have gone through to create this work of art?" Seeing other people's work reminds me that crafting something beautiful takes time and patience.

Your job today is not to think about work, but to have a sensory aesthetic experience. Do not try to think about your writing. Let the art affect you on a subconscious level. You will learn, through osmosis, lessons about deliberation and spontaneity, about passion and the role of art in history. Let the experience feed your spirit and your work will flow from there.

My sister Julia suggests going someplace familiar at an unfamiliar time. The supermarket takes on a different air after midnight, and you can see the colorful design of the produce displays. I love to walk through downtown San Francisco when the town is asleep for the night; you might visit a commercial district before the residents are awake, or a night spot in the middle of the day.

NPR commentator and poet Andrei Codrescu likes to go to the zoo not only to observe the animals, but also to watch the humans interact. You might try visiting a botanical garden, an amusement park or even a cemetery. Pay attention to the emotions these places elicit in you and in other visitors. Attend a sporting event you'd normally avoid. Observe and absorb the concentrated energy generated by the players and the crowd.

An unfamiliar house of worship—a church, temple, mosque, shrine, or synagogue—can be a wonderful place to discover new experiences. As an outsider, you can observe the serenity and depth of other faiths or the collective spirit of the congregation. Perhaps you can find someone to explain how the ritual objects are used or what the various symbols mean. Ask questions about the group's beliefs and you may come to better understand the power of story and the way it can influence generations.

"**I** apparently have to dawdle a certain amount before I go to work," wrote John Steinbeck in a letter to his friend and publisher, Pascal Covici. In fact, one of the ways Steinbeck dawdled most effectively was by writing letters. Every morning, as a kind of warm up, Steinbeck would write Covici a letter (unmailed) in the oversized notebook that contained the growing manuscript of *East of Eden*. He explained this process as a way of getting his "mental arm in shape to pitch a good game." These let-

write a

Letter

ters were a kind of "arguing ground" for the story as well as a place to voice the fears, ambitions, and preoccupations that might otherwise interfere with his work.

A number of chapters in *East of Eden* actually started out as letters Steinbeck wrote to his sons, Tom and John. In later drafts he dropped the direct salutations, but the act of writing to people he loved helped Steinbeck find both the message and the proper tone for the novel.

Many books start out as letters to loved ones. *House of the Spirits* began as a letter from Isabel Allende to her ninety-nine-year-old grandfather. Ray Bradbury's short story "Calling Mexico" evolved from a note directed to a distant pal. Katherine Anne Porter realized she had the beginning of a novel, *Ship of Fools*, when she reread the packet of letters she had sent a friend as a sort of shipboard diary.

Ralph Waldo Emerson used to write a friend whenever he was feeling stuck. Sue Grafton employs a similar technique but writes directly to her subconscious mind. Opening with the words *Dear Right Brain*, she states the problem she is trying to solve, asks *"R. B."* for help, and signs off *Your pal, Sue*. Grafton's right brain seems to like these notes as it often wakes her in the middle of the night with answers to her questions.

Inspired by these authors, I began to start my writing day with a letter. For years I opened with the words *Dear Bessie*, addressing an aunt who died before I was born, and ended with the words *Love, N.* In between I'd unload the thoughts and feelings that might otherwise clog my brain. Nowadays I leave off the salutation but rarely start the day without a letter or journal entry.

Rather than going directly to the task of writing for an unseen audience, try addressing your thoughts to a friend. This can be someone real or imaginary. Ground your thoughts on paper so that they don't clutter your mind.

If you are stuck in your work, write a letter describing your current dilemma. Outline what you are trying to accomplish and name the obstacles in your way. As you write about this thing you want to do, you may very well find it taking shape right there on the paper.

Writing a letter helps relieve unnecessary pressure. You don't have to create perfect prose, you are simply playing. And out of your attempt to understand and communicate, new ideas and the words to express them will emerge.

One of the hardest jobs in creating *Writers Dreaming* was enticing famous writers to talk with me. I needed to establish my credentials, impress them with my knowledge, and explain the benefits they would derive from speaking with me—all in less than a page!

It took four letters and one year to get Stephen King to agree to an interview. When I found myself struggling for the right words, I'd write myself a letter, exploring what I needed to say and experimenting with form. "I'm trying to get King to talk to me," I'd write. "I know he doesn't need to do this interview for publicity, but maybe he'd do it because. . . ." With these words I started sketching out the reasons why he would want to talk. Gradually the note began to compose itself. I was then able to copy the letter within the letter, revise it, and put it in the mail.

If there is a letter you have been meaning to write—to gather information, obtain permission, or sell an idea—take time to do it now. You can work your way into the text by starting it as a note to yourself.

Is there someone from your past that you would like to write today? A friend? A teacher? A former spouse? Express the things you were never able to tell this person. Share some of the insights you've gained since your last communication. You need not mail this letter—simply voice your thoughts and feelings on paper. You may come to understand an unresolved issue that has blocked your progress or haunted one of your characters.

find the Need

According to novelist Kurt Vonnegut, the fault with most amateur writing is a lack of character motivation. "Make your characters want something right away," he advises. "Even if it's only a glass of water. Even characters paralyzed by the meaninglessness of life have to have a glass of water from time to time."

National Book Award–winning author Robert Olen Butler concurs. "Human beings are constantly yearning. Every moment we are wanting something. Even if the desire is not to desire. Or if the desire is to desire." Butler believes the writer's job is to find the yearning at the "white hot center" of his or her own being and to connect with a character on that level.

If you're looking for a new story to tell, identify a personal longing and embody it in a character very different from yourself. Butler created the powerful story "Snow" by placing his own longing for love into the person of a Vietnamese waitress alone in an empty Louisiana restaurant on Christmas Eve.

Whether you are writing fiction, history, or biography, determine what each of your characters needs. What are their long-term needs—to avenge a wrong? To achieve financial security? To break a draining emotional attachment? What are their immediate physical needs—to get to a bathroom? To dispose of a body? To retrieve a document?

In an interview in the *Paris Review*, Kurt Vonnegut described a student's story about a nun who got a piece of dental floss caught between two molars. "The story dealt with issues a lot more important than dental floss, but what kept readers going was anxiety about when the dental floss would finally be removed. Nobody could read that story without fishing around in his mouth with a finger."

Create an incident that illustrates one of your character's unspoken needs. If he needs money, show him scrounging for food in a supermarket dumpster or checking the coin return slots of pay telephones. If she is trying to hide her alcoholism, have her shop at different liquor stores each time she needs booze or pretend to be having a party when she orders wine from room service.

When you feel stuck, stop and ask yourself what your character needs right now: "How can I show her trying to get it? If she needs attention, would she say something provocative at a party? Shoplift underwear? Cut herself with a knife?"

Tristine Ranier, author of *Your Life As Story*, suggests that, in memoir as well as in fiction, motivation must be a constant element: "The character [you] should have a clear desire line. It can bend, it can turn unexpectedly, but it should not break. It should be intense and continuous. As soon as one need is met, another appears."

Ranier uses the Cinderella story to illustrate the changing but continuous nature of desire. First Cinderella has a desire to be liked and accepted by her stepsisters. Then she wants to go to the ball, wear a beautiful gown, and dance with the prince. Next she needs to escape by midnight without being discovered. Finally her desire is to try on the slipper so she can be united with the prince and escape from her wicked stepfamily.

Map out a character's desire line on a piece of paper. Note the places where, for instance, it changes from desire for a job to desire for a particular job, then to desiring a corner office, a raise, and so on. Find incidents that illustrate the various stages of desire as they are challenged by conflicting needs or circumstances.

To create a mystery novel, you have to assemble a number of suspects, each one displaying a different need. Edgar Award–winning author Julie Smith uses a kind of game to make the plotting process fun. First she generates a list of motives—jealousy, revenge, greed, etc. She then creates a cast of characters, each driven by a different motive. Suspect number one might have wanted to kill the victim, a compulsive gambler, because he had stolen her money. Suspect two might have wanted to kill the victim because he was sleeping with his wife. Suspect three might be the wife who would have killed to hide the adultery from her husband. All of these characters are put into place to fill the needs of the reader—whose desire is to figure out who did the dirty deed.

It is important to identify your own needs as a writer so that the writing process can serve a deep purpose inside you. When I began *Writers Dreaming,* it was not just to know what successful writers dreamt about, but to fill my own desire to become more creative. I would not have been able to sustain interest in the project for so many years had I not been working to answer a personal need.

Make a list of the questions you most want answered, the issues you need to explore. Use your writing to discover how other people might have dealt with a problem or satisfied a desire.

Susan Page began to write the best-selling *If I'm So Wonderful Why Am I Still Single?* to figure out why she was single herself. As she wrote she came to understand some of the factors that kept so many wonderful people from finding life partners. She developed exercises to help deal with fear and ambivalence. And, in so doing, she found Mayer Shacter, whom she married before the book was complete.

If a subject has power for you, there are probably readers who will welcome your work. I was able to sell *Writers Dreaming* to a publisher because I established in my proposal the need that the book would fill in others—the need to understand the creative process so that we can be more creative ourselves.

Think about the needs your work will fill for others. Determine who your audience really is. Are you writing for someone like yourself who needs encouragement? Are you writing to warn a specific population of some concrete danger? Are you writing to explain some phenomenon to a group of novices, or are you trying to reach a sophisticated audience? Knowing who you are writing for will give your work more focus. It will also replace the need (and fear) of impressing other people and give you a sense of purpose.

"Thrust your hand deep into life, and whatever you bring up in it, that is your subject," said the poet Goethe. Let's take Goethe's suggestion literally—thrust your hand into a pocket or a drawer and use the first object you touch as a subject for your writing.

You may pull out a common household item—a pair of scissors, a stamp, a box of crayons. Whatever you find has a history and a purpose. Imagine other hands that might have handled this object and the role

open a

Drawer

it might have played in someone else's life. Let what you find trigger your imagination. Write a scene in which this object plays a crucial part.

It is in the secret places—pockets, drawers, purses, closets, safety deposit boxes—that the hidden life of a character is revealed.

In his autobiography *Rewrites*, Neil Simon remembers reaching into the pockets of his father's overcoat. "I could feel the cellophane worn off a pack of cigarettes, a matchbook, a pencil, a single Lifesaver, a paper clip, bits of tobacco, all giving me a hint and smell of what his day was like."

My mother recently pulled a key from the catch-all drawer in her kitchen. She found herself remembering a package she'd received almost fifty years earlier, sent by a boyfriend stationed abroad during World War II. Enclosed was a key he'd found on the battlefield. This inspired an ardent correspondence in which they both speculated about who the key had belonged to and what it had opened.

Imagine what someone—a real person or a fictional character—might be carrying in his wallet or hiding in her underwear drawer. Make a list of the items you've imagined, then write a page inspired by one of them.

As Goethe told Johann Peter Eckerman, "At bottom, no real object is unpoetical." So explore finding poetry in the mundane.

Stretch your understanding of metaphor by picking an object and comparing it to one of your characters. How is he or she like a three-pronged electrical adaptor? Does he have two sides to his personality, one that takes in stimuli and another that sends it out? Is she a passive receptor? A transformer of input? Does she act as a conduit for the energy of others? Can he help ground another's electrical current?

You might want to compare the object you've chosen to an abstract concept. How is love like an electrical adaptor? How does money serve that same function?

Take a look at the e. e. cummings poem "She Being Brand New" to see how the poet described a sexual experience in vivid, uncensorable detail by casting one partner as an automobile. Using automotive terms, cummings managed to created an auto-erotic masterpiece.

Title

What you name a piece of writing can make an important difference in how it is perceived. As Samuel Butler once remarked, "*The Rhyme of the Ancient Mariner* would not have taken off so well had it been called The Old Sailor."

"The title is vital," says novelist Daniel Reveles. The names of his books—*Enchiladas, Rice and Beans*, and *Salsa and Chips*—immediately alert potential readers to their simple ethnic flavor.

"The title always comes first, to me and to the reader," Guillermo Cabrera Infante told the *Paris Review*. "I've written many stories and articles just by doggedly following the title." Even so, Infante sometimes replaces the original name of a piece when it is done.

Richard Paul Evans began his bestselling novels *The Christmas Box* and *The Time Piece* knowing only what they would be called.

Brainstorm a list of titles for a piece you'd like to write. Don't censor yourself—let them be funny, silly, poetic, strange. Then pick one and let it lead you to a story.

Singer and songwriter Elton John likes to extract phrases from people's sentences and turn them into titles. If audio engineer Rod Duggan remarked about the beauty of the shadows on the lawn, John might suddenly interrupt the conversation, saying "Shadows on the Lawn by Rod Duggan, a romantic comedy" or "Beauty of the Shadows, a tragedy in three acts."

If you are searching for a title for your work, enlist the aid of several friends and have a brainstorming session. Use a thesaurus to generate a list of words. Consult a book of quotations for evocative phrases.

Neil Simon likes to take phrases that are already part of the language. He chose *Come Blow Your Horn*, *The Odd Couple*, *The Last of the Red Hot Lovers*, and *The Star Spangled Girl* because they sound familiar and are easy to remember. Tennessee Williams told the *Paris Review* he often found titles by looking through the poetry of Hart Crane.

Create a list of chapter titles to guide you through a project. This will help you determine its scope and content, as well as its tone. If you are planning to write nonfiction, this is an easy first step in preparing a book proposal.

When writing his memoir, my father was able to stay motivated by referring back to a list of chapter titles he'd generated for a class. The teacher prompted ideas with simple phrases like "my most unforgettable character," "my worst day at work," and "my first love." Make yourself a list of phrases like these to inspire future work.

Jeremy Taylor, author of *Dream Work* and *Where People Fly and Water Runs Uphill*, also suggests giving your dreams and nightmares titles to help you remember them. Try doing this with an event in your own life. Once you have crystallized a title, a story might suddenly emerge.

"The eraser is as important as the pencil," says composer Billy Charlap. The silences in music, as in conversation, are as vital as the notes. To produce your finest work, you have to be willing to eliminate excess words, characters, subplots, and even ideas.

In order to get thoughts flowing and discover what you have to say, you must always write more than you use. Louis-Ferdinand Celine (*Death on the Installment Plan*, *Journey to the End of the Night*) made

eliminate

Words

this clear when he said, "To do a novel like one of mine you have to write 80,000 pages in order to get 800."

Allow yourself to write garbage, to repeat yourself, to produce clichés. Let yourself create what Anne Lamott calls "shitty first drafts." Bad writing is part of the creative process. Besides, you are going to need to generate some lousy material in order to have something to revise.

It took Neil Simon a year to write the first draft of *Come Blow Your Horn* and two and a half years to revise it. He would start each draft at the beginning and work through until the end. "There was barely any similarity between the first draft and the twenty-second. The play was so primitive in its earliest versions, it bordered on Neanderthal."

Simon likes to put a draft into a drawer for several weeks before rereading it. "At that point the words no longer seem to come from me but rather it's as though some unknown person has sent it to me through the mail, asking my opinion of it. As I read it, what's good remains good, but what's bad jumps off the page and smacks me right across my ego. My thick black indelible pen puts a line through every inferior word and sentence, blocking it out forever for any theater historian who might find it one day and say 'My God! How could he write such crap?'"

Kurt Vonnegut tells students to "start on page three," where the action really begins. Eliminate excess exposition—when the character was born, where he grew up, how he got to work that day. These are things you may have needed to write to ease yourself into the story, but they may not be things your readers need to know.

Irwin Shaw says that "the last paragraph in which you tell what the story is about is almost always best left out." Shaw learned this painful lesson after several of his stories were truncated by editors at the *New Yorker*.

Take a piece of unfinished work and skim it without judgment. (If you have nothing available, free-write for twenty minutes and use the results.) Your task is simply to see what's there. Now go back and circle the parts you like the best. Where you've been redundant, cross it out. Note in the margins places where you need to clarify, condense, rearrange, or expand. Then retype the corrected pages, incorporating your suggestions. You will probably find yourself making more improvements as you go along. Henry Miller once said, "The mere mechanical business of touching the keys sharpens my thoughts and I find myself revising while doing the finished thing."

"If in doubt, throw it out" is what painter Phyllis Murphy used to say to me. Neil Simon echoes this sentiment: "You can never say to yourself, 'I think there's a problem here but maybe I'm wrong. Maybe they'll like it.' They won't. They barely like it when you think it's wonderful, so what chance do you have when you try to slip something in that even you have doubts about?"

Sometimes the things you have to eliminate are actually words that you love. "It's no use putting in nice lines that you think are good poetry if they don't get the action on at all," T. S. Eliot once said about the creation of *Murder in the Cathedral*.

"The very bitter lesson that everyone who wants to write has got to learn, is that a thing may in itself be the finest piece of writing one has ever done, and yet have absolutely no place in the manuscript one hopes to publish." It was with this realization that Thomas Wolfe deleted a scene in *Of Time and the River* that he'd spent months writing.

You can sometimes take work cut from one piece and use it in another. Susan Page was distraught when told that she'd have to eliminate half of her ideas from *If I'm So Wonderful, Why Am I Still Single?* But after cutting things out, she realized she had enough material to start a second book—and a third, fourth, and fifth.

Like many authors, Patricia MacLachlan never throws anything away. She has a special file where she stores excised material. Ellen Ullman *(Close to the Machine)* refers to this place as "the bone pile," (a term she got from Sandy Emerson). It can serve as a fabulous source of new ideas. As T. S. Eliot told the *Paris Review*, *Burnt Norton* began with bits he'd cut from *Murder in the Cathedral*.

Sometimes you need to eliminate a character to make your work more effective. In creating his novel *The Blood Countess*, Andrei Codrescu realized that two of his characters were serving the same function. So he combined them into one. A deleted character may resurface in another story, or may in fact deserve a story of its own.

Dale Carnegie cautioned public speakers to beware of "weasel words." Phrases like "it seems to me, perhaps, in my opinion" were given this name by Theodore Roosevelt because "the weasel sucks the heart out of an egg and leaves nothing but the empty shell."

Comb through a manuscript to eliminate excess verbiage. "One word for two" is the phrase overseas development specialist Michael Mercil uses to help people write.

When Ernest Hemingway was challenged to write a short story in as few words as possible, he needed only six words: "For sale. Baby shoes. Never worn."

If you have nothing to revise today, see if you can create a story in less than ten words. Or try this exercise designed by Sue Pace for the Willamette Writers Conference: Create a story title by combining a color and a noun (for example, The Black Dog or The Green Sponge). Now take a few minutes to write a piece of no more than 100 words. Retell the story from another character's point of view and then eliminate twenty words. You'd think that with only 100 words you'd produce a pretty tight piece. But eliminating 20 percent makes the writing so much better. Now eliminate another twenty words and see what you've got. You may see a vast improvement, and you may have just created something you'd like to develop further.

Years ago, when I was desperately searching for a way to channel my creative energies, Susan Page (*If I'm So Wonderful Why Am I Still Single?*) and I decided to create our own mini-self-help program. A friend loaned us a series of motivation tapes he'd purchased from an infomercial, swearing that they really worked. We figured we could ignore the hyperbole and bluster of the TV guru and still learn something. So we agreed to meet every morning at 7 A.M., listen to the tapes,

Breathe

and do the exercises. At least we'd have a reason to get up early.

There was a lot of You too can have ultimate power and own helicopters like me on the tapes, but there were also some very potent suggestions. One of the most valuable exercises had us spend a few minutes, two times a day, simply breathing. We were to inhale on the count of five, hold for a count of twenty and then exhale on a count of ten. This whole process took only three minutes, but you cannot imagine how resistant I was to spending even this amount of time outside my normal frantic state.

Those breathing breaks allowed me to slow down and open up so that new thoughts could emerge. Two weeks into the breathing program, I began to write the words that evolved into my first book, *Writers Dreaming.*

Breathing also helped me name this deck. It was originally called Creative Openings, then one day I decided to quiet down, close my eyes, and breathe. As I sat cross-legged on my bed, paying attention to nothing but my breath, the words *Observation Deck* popped into my mind.

Mystery writer Sue Grafton combines a simple mantra with the focused breathing she often does to begin her work day. As she breathes in and out she feeds herself the suggestion that she will be "productive, energetic, and imaginative," and that she will solve whatever problem she is currently facing. You might want to adapt Grafton's words or create your own simple saying to repeat with every breath.

Ira Progoff, creator of the Intensive Journal Workshop, suggests you take a powerful personal image and create a seven-syllable phrase, like "holding the stillness within," or "the waters beyond the well." This is not a sentence with a subject and an object but rather a fragment that evokes a peaceful or powerful state of mind. With each complete cycle of inhale and exhale you repeat the phrase so the words ride on the movement of air.

The word *inspiration* comes from the Latin root *spirare*, to breathe. It also contains the root of the word *spirit.*

When you feel stuck or are looking for inspiration, take a few minutes to breathe. Flush out old, tired ideas by exhaling fully. As you inhale, imagine that you are aerating your blood, sending fresh oxygen to every cell. Concentrate on the physical sensation of air moving through your nose and lungs, expanding and contracting. Use this as a time to focus your thoughts on a seemingly effortless action.

Jon Kabat Zinn, author of *Wherever You Go, There You Are*, calls the breath "an anchor line to tether you to the present moment." Since the best time to create is now, let conscious breathing help you center yourself in the present so that you can write.

Play around with different ways of breathing. Breathe as if you are suffering from emphysema. Breathe as if you're a robust hiker taking in fresh mountain air. Breathe like a haughty aristocrat, a flighty, birdlike woman, or a raging bull. As you try out various ways of breathing, you may gain new insight into the way a character feels in different situations.

variations

Many of us harbor an image of a writer as someone who sits at a desk, typing away. We feel that unless we are in a similar position, we cannot be effective. But many writers get their ideas while walking, swimming, or bathing and put words onto paper while standing up or lying down.

Robert Frost used to sit in an overstuffed chair with a writing board across his lap. Thomas Wolfe often wrote standing up, using the top of his refrigerator as a desk. Hemingway also wrote standing, his type-

Move

writer perched on top of his dresser. Mozart used to transcribe in bed, a place also used by Pulitzer Prize winner Daniel Yergin and children's poet Jack Prelutsky.

Computer book maven Bob Cowart recommends writing in bed because "you have all the comforts of the womb. You don't have to worry what to wear and besides, it keeps the blood closer to the brain."

Truman Capote claimed he couldn't think unless he was lying down, either in bed or stretched out on a couch with cigarettes and coffee handy. "I've got to be puffing and sipping," he told the *Paris Review*. "As the afternoon wears on, I shift from coffee to mint tea to sherry to martinis."

It is much easier for me to start the writing day if I don't get out of bed until I have written for at least half an hour. Once I have showered, dressed, eaten, and walked the dog, my energy is scattered. Henriette Klauser, author of *Writing on Both Sides of the Brain*, helped me understand that it is better to start writing before your inner critic wakes up—postponing the usual morning rituals gives the critic within the illusion that he or she can leave you unattended.

Experiment with finding the best position for yourself. Sitting at a desk may help get the ideas flowing, but if you find yourself stuck, try something new. Write standing up. Write lying down.

Take a shower or bath. Virginia Woolf conceived one of her novels in the bathtub. Douglas Adams, author of *The Hitchhikers Guide to the Universe*, jumps into the tub whenever he is stuck. Filmmaker and novelist John Sayles gets ideas while swimming in the pool.

Exercise. Put on some music and dance.

Irving Stone has said that when he has trouble writing, he steps out into the garden and pulls weeds. Carol Shields vacuums. Many people think that cleaning house is a way to avoid writing, but Shields assures us that getting your space straightened out can be an essential preliminary to settling down to work.

Some of us need the energy of other people to be productive. Natalie Goldberg, author of *Writing Down the Bones*, recommends writing in cafes. Ernest Hemingway composed *The Sun Also Rises* in hotel rooms, cafes, and bars in several cities. Bob Cowart, when he does get out of bed, carries his laptop to different libraries around Berkeley, California, or jumps onto his scooter and travels from cafe to cafe to write.

Scott Turow used to write his novels riding the train from his home in the suburbs to his law office in Chicago. The movement of the train and the time-limited structure helped him work. Well after Turow had retired from his law practice, he continued riding the rails to write.

NPR commentator, poet, and novelist Andrei Codrescu likes to go to cities where he knows absolutely no one and write. So does

Lawrence Block, who holes up in hotels for six-week stretches when he needs to complete a book.

Since a trip to another city or country may not be possible today, go to a different place or find a different way to work right now.

Take something you have been working on, choose an unfamiliar position, and work for fifteen minutes. If you do not have a current project, choose an *Observation Deck* card at random and write about that topic. If you pull the "Squint" card, write about squinting. If you happen to pull the "Study Opening Lines" card, write about the opening line someone used in a conversation. Or write about your plans for the day. See how the change in position affects the way your words flow.

If you've got a scene that isn't quite working, move your characters to a new location or change their physical positions in relation to one another. Have a dialogue take place in a strange bedroom, late at night where people in the next room might overhear; in a vehicle, driving under dangerous conditions; or during a guided tour of some unusual site.

Play with where and how you deliver your exposition. In John Berendt's *Midnight in the Garden of Good and Evil*, a character shares interesting bits of Savannah history while sipping cocktails in a graveyard. In *Get Shorty*, Elmore Leonard reveals bits of his heroine's background as she stands listening for a prowler at the top of a staircase.

If you're writing a screenplay, it is especially important to set your action in visually interesting locations. This constraint can actually help you add layers of meaning to a scene. In the movie *Quiz Show,* writer Paul Attanasio communicates several things at once by setting a conversation in an outdoor phone booth. We learn from the dialogue that contestant Mark Van Doren is about to be investigated for cheating, while we witness the downside of his growing fame as fans besiege the booth demanding autographs.

We learn something extra about two characters when a business meeting takes place, not in an office, but in a living room, with one character riding an exercise bike and the other holding his towel. If a falling-in-love scene is set in an amusement park, a writer might foreshadow a dramatic moment by demonstrating the man's vulnerability to being conned as well as the woman's fear of heights.

Create a scene in a new environment. Make that environment extreme. High up on a mountaintop, deep down in a mine, way out on a country road. Set your scene in a factory, a shopping mall, a dentist's chair. Put your characters in unusual positions—working beneath a car or reaching for something while standing on a chair. By placing physical constraints on a character, you increase the dramatic effect of your words.

"It's the writer's job to stage confrontations so the characters will say surprising and revealing things," says novelist Kurt Vonnegut. "If a writer can't or won't do that, he should withdraw from the trade."

Pulitzer Prize–winning novelist Robert Penn Warren makes the point more bluntly: "No conflict, no story." John LeCarre furnishes an example: "The cat sat on the mat is not a story. The cat sat on the other cat's mat is a story."

In fiction the conflict can be internal or

create a Conflict

external, but it must manifest itself in action. It can be a war of values fought within an individual or a battle of wills between two or more people. The conflict can occur between institutions or ways of thinking, but it must be shown through human action.

In LeCarre's novels the conflict is never just a fight between superpowers. Individuals are not only pitted against one another—the hero is usually also engaged in an internal battle, torn between personal and institutional loyalty. Conscious of irreconcilable differences within himself, LeCarre searches his own inner conflicts for material to explore in his books.

If you are writing nonfiction, be aware that you are battling with old ideas in your presentation of new ones. Keep the opposing arguments in mind so that you can address them fully.

Identify the conflict in the piece you are writing. It probably exists on several levels—internal, external, societal. Create an incident that allows some conflict to erupt in action. Fan the flames, up the ante, make the danger bigger and see what happens.

If you want to start a new piece, make a list of conflicts operating both in our society and in your life. Pick one that has great charge for you and find a way to illustrate it dramatically. Create a scene in which opposing forces can do battle. Give your ideas names and faces and let them duke it out. For an essay, start with an anecdote that illuminates a clash in values.

To see how conflict works in literature, look at a favorite story and see how many levels of conflict you can find. Study the ways in which the author makes internal conflicts manifest in action.

If you feel stuck in your work, write about the forces that are at war within you. Give each force a voice and let them fight things out. Allow perfectionism to face off against your desire to coast. Pit fear of failure against fear of success. Let the opposing forces argue on paper until some other voice appears to mediate the conflict. I did this once with the part of me that loves to eat and the part that thinks I'll get fat if I don't stop eating. After several pages of name calling, a new character whom I call the briefcase lady appeared and worked out a brilliant compromise. She said I could take food home in a doggie bag so I wouldn't feel deprived and could save the calories for another day. Your inner voices have important information to give you, if you just let them have their say.

Late one night in Savannah, as John Berendt struggled with a difficult piece of writing, he found himself reaching for the telephone. It was too late to call any friends, so he dialed his Manhattan apartment. When the machine answered he read into the phone, hung up, and then hit redial. Hearing his words echoing back across 1,000 miles, Berendt suddenly understood how to improve them. In fact, the act of reading into the phone had caused him to spontaneously correct for rhythm and flow.

Read Aloud

Berendt continued this long distance relationship throughout the writing of *Midnight in the Garden of Good and Evil,* a book that would spend more than three years on the *New York Times* best-seller list.

For many writers, reading aloud is an essential step in the creative process. Tennessee Williams vocalized as he wrote. Kingsley Amis waited until the end of the day and read his work to his wife. Truman Capote would put his writing aside for weeks, even months, and then read it aloud to friends.

"I pace," says Allan Gurganus, author of *The Oldest Living Confederate Widow Tells All.* "I live alone and my neighbors think I have a very active and busy apartment. But all the voices are me and mine or us and ours. . . ." Before publication, Gurganus reads aloud everything he writes thirty or forty times, because "there's a kind of ear music that operates as an editorial principle on the page . . . a rhythmic synchronicity which pulls [readers] into the fiction and creates a kind of heartbeat on the page."

Echo Heron, a nurse in a critical care unit, used reading aloud to anticipate and avoid criticism of what was to become her best-selling memoir, *Intensive Care.* After completing each draft, she closed the curtains, assumed a British accent, and read to an imaginary audience made up of people she wanted to impress. Fear of negative reactions forced her to automatically correct poor grammar and sloppy thinking as she read. New lines erupted spontaneously as she saw the need to furnish missing concepts.

Right now, choose a piece of writing to read out loud. If your work is on the computer, be sure to print it out instead of reading off the screen. Don't be embarrassed if it sounds a bit awkward—reading aloud will help improve the flow. You might, like Echo Heron, adopt a foreign accent or assume a new persona to create distance and avoid self-consciousness. Or you can follow novelist Elizabeth Berg's example and tape-record your reading, then lie down—in the bath or on the sofa—and listen to the replay. You might read to a friend over the telephone or use a neighbor as a sounding board. Keep a pencil handy, since you'll want to mark down any spontaneous changes you make as you read. To gain critical distance, you can also have a friend read your work aloud to you. If you are working on a play or a screenplay, invite several friends over to help you hear what works and what can be improved. Be clear that what they are reading is a work-in-progress and not something to be judged as complete.

"Verbalizing is one of the best critical procedures," said novelist Robertson Davies. "If you meet with a passage in a book that seems to you to be, in some way, dubious or false, try reading it aloud and your doubts will be settled. The trick of argument or falsity of emphasis will declare itself to your ear, when it seems to be deceiving your eye."

Davies recommends that you read good literature out loud, or at least slowly enough to verbalize every word. "When you are reading," he says "you cannot save time, but you can diminish your pleasure by trying to do so." You can also miss the subtleties that make great writing great. Reading slowly, you sensitize your ear and automatically work to achieve more depth, nuance, and precision.

For more than twenty-five years, my mother has been stimulating her intellect while helping others as a volunteer reader with Recording for the Blind and Dyslexic. She has learned about new developments in psychology, sociology, and grammar. In college I earned extra money by reading texts onto tape for a blind classmate. Not only did I make a new friend, but through this process I was able to absorb the material much more efficiently.

Read to a child, a lover, a pet. Savor the texture of the words in your mouth and share your pleasure with another.

Use reading others' work aloud as a way to jump-start your own writing. Let the rhythm and sound of the work carry you to the point where you are ready to let your own words flow onto paper. Then write for ten minutes.

And remember, whenever you are writing dialogue, take John Steinbeck's advice: "Say it aloud as you write it. Only then will it have the sound of speech."

follow the Scent

In 1995, I lost the ability to smell. I didn't notice its absence until a perfumer friend asked me to praise her newest concoction. She didn't believe me when I said I could not smell a thing. But it was true. A year later when, thanks to modern medicine, my sense of smell returned, I was chagrined to discover that my car, which I use to drive authors to signings, readings, and interviews, smelled a bit like my dog.

I gained a new appreciation of odors, both good and bad. I could now smell jasmine and honeysuckle, coffee and strawberries, rotting food in the fridge, leather, ink, and leaking gas.

The nose is an early warning system as well as an organ of pleasure. It has the power to evoke lost memories and activate frozen emotions.

Goethe is reported to have peeked into the poet Schiller's desk drawer only to find it filled with rotting apples. Daring to inquire, Goethe learned that whenever Schiller was blocked, he simply opened the drawer, smelled its contents, and the flow of words returned.

Think about the smells that have seasoned your life. Hot cocoa, green tea, fresh lemons. The strongest scent memories I have evoke my childhood. The sulfurous odor of cooked cabbage in the stairwell of an old Detroit apartment building. Steaming chocolate pudding awaiting my return from dancing in the rain in my bathing suit. The stinging combination of bleach, urine, and rubbing alcohol that permeates a hospital room.

Recalling the pink, plastic-wrapped deodorizer that hung from a wire inside my grandmother's toilet, I am instantly transported back in time, staring at the black-and-white octagonal tiles that lined the bathroom floor.

Brylcream, English Leather, Old Spice, and stale tobacco bring back memories of different men in different eras. Patchouli oil, incense, and marijuana evoke the 1960s. The intoxicating smell of rubber cement brings back memories of sitting on the basement floor gluing colored paper, getting high while making art.

For screenwriter Sue Mittelman, it's the scent of burning leaves; for biochemist Helen Revel it's the smell of fresh mown hay; for novelist W. E. Reinka, it's the fumes of airplane glue—each brings childhood imagery flooding back. Jennifer Futura turned her memories into a powerful personal essay when she realized how she had always associated Pine Sol with rich people's homes.

Make a list of twenty-five smells—pleasant and unpleasant, natural and industrial. Choose one as a writing catalyst and let it trigger images, thoughts, and feelings.

Do a little sniffing around your house. Go into your kitchen and smell some spices. Visit the bathroom and open some jars.

Think about the smells you associate with a loved one. Mothballs, perfume, the scent of his or her skin. Let the memory of this fragrance inspire you to write.

If you are currently working on a piece, think about the smells you might find in your character's world. Search them out and smell them for yourself. Bring these odors into your story.

Right Name

Novelist Clyde Edgerton was driving through rural Mississippi when he passed a sign for Uncle Babe's Launderette. Suddenly he realized that one of his characters had failed to take on life because he'd been given the wrong name. Edgerton immediately rechristened the character Uncle Babe and the book took off.

Sometimes a piece of writing stalls simply because a character has been misnamed. Children's book author Madeleine L'Engle *(A Wrinkle in Time)* struggled with a novel that wouldn't work until she changed the name of one of her characters. As soon as Ben became Simon, several references she had made unconsciously made sense and the writing of *Dragons in the Waters* began to flow.

"Names are magical," said novelist John Gardner. "If you name a kid John, he'll grow up a different kid than if you name him Rudolf." In *The Language of Names,* Justin Kaplan and Anne Bernays revealed that in early drafts of *A Christmas Carol,* Tiny Tim was called Little Larry, Small Sam, and Punky Pete.

Names can be found in all sorts of places. Newbery Award–winning author Patricia

MacLachlan was having a difficult time with a book when a little boy approached her at a reading. He introduced himself as Journey, and she immediately asked if she could use his name. Once she had given her hero this evocative moniker, the novel *Journey* practically wrote itself.

Dorothy Parker found character names in phone books and obituaries. Clyde Edgerton uses these same sources, but he divides the names into two columns—one of first names, one of last names—and makes new combinations.

Brainstorm a list of interesting names or pick one from the phone book. Then sketch a written portrait of the person who might bear such a name. Assign her an age, occupation, and marital status. Describe his hobbies, mode of dress, and favorite foods. Think of three other names such a person might bear.

variations

Nobel Prize–winning author Jorge Luis Borges liked to work the names of his ancestors into his writing. He felt this gave them a kind of immortality.

Is there someone whose name you would like to immortalize? W. E. Reinka named a body of water Lake Naomi to give me a thrill. In his novel *If I Never Get Back*, Darryl Brock called a steamboat the *MaryRae* to honor his friend MaryRae Thewlis. By injecting a loved one or someone you admire into your writing you can give yourself a new source of inspiration.

Leslie Marmon Silko was already four years into the writing of *The Almanac of the Dead* when her MacArthur Prize money ran out. The novel was nowhere near finished, but her attention was being distracted by the blank wall outside her window. So she left her desk, went outside, and began to paint a mural. She covered the forty-foot width of the wall with a giant snake whose belly was full of skulls, adding some words in Spanish about revolution. The act of painting freed Marmon Silko's

Switch Media

mind and helped her find an ending to the novel.

Sometimes it is important to switch media—to paint or dance or sculpt or sing. Let the energy that is not coming out in your writing find other outlets.

Take time today to play in another medium. Find magic markers, paint, or clay. Make a collage with bits of paper torn from magazines. Use art materials to explore a question or amplify an image. What you create may seem totally unrelated to your work, but then, even Marmon Silko didn't realize the importance of her snake until long after she had painted its image. Looking back, she understood that the snake had been embedded in her book from the beginning and held an important message for the story.

When I'm feeling stuck, I often draw cartoons of my alter-ego Lula. She is a simple line drawing: one line for hair, two dots for eyes, two hands, and two feet. If she has something she wants to say, I put the words in a bubble. Sometimes she tells me I'm working too hard. Sometimes she tells me I need to do more. Sometimes I bring other stick figures into the frame and engage Lula in conversation. In this way various parts of my psyche find expression, and I often gain startling new insights.

Some people love to work out their tensions by molding images out of plasticine or candle wax. They avoid getting attached to the outcome because every few minutes they can make their work disappear, remolding it into another sculptural form. Try something equally impermanent—art for relaxation's sake rather than for display.

Perhaps you find creative release in cooking or gardening or arranging flowers. When technical writer Bob Cowart is feeling stuck, he gets up and plays the piano. Novelist Mark Salzman pulls out his cello. Sue Bender, author of *Plain and Simple*, makes pots out of clay. When he wasn't writing, John Steinbeck used to build wood furniture in order to relax and unwind.

If you are currently working on a story, you may want to translate one element into another medium. Sketch, paint, or sculpt one character; design a piece of clothing; draw a city map or create a floor plan of a family home. Do a watercolor that depicts the season or hum a melody that evokes the mood of a scene.

You may want to pretend you are one of your characters while you create some sort of art. Draw a picture, pound the piano, build a sand castle, or fill in a coloring book and you will gain insight and empathy as you play.

observe a

Ritual

Every Friday, just after sunset, my mother lights two candles to welcome in the Jewish Sabbath. This begins a twenty-four-hour period in which the mundane tasks of the work week are set aside in favor of friends, family, and regeneration. This day of rest is intended to be a complete departure from daily routines. Saturday evening, when three stars appear in the sky, a blue and white braided candle is lit, signaling a return to ordinary life.

Rituals delineate time, setting boundaries so that when it is time to work, we can really focus and when it is time to celebrate or mourn, we can do so fully. Rituals help us shift gears, make transitions, change our mental states.

Many writers have rituals to begin and end the writing day. These may be conscious acts designed to invoke a muse or unconscious routines which, like Pavlovian stimuli, trigger a mindset conducive to work.

Jack Kerouac used to light a candle to start each writing session and blow it out when he was through. Willa Cather read a passage from the Bible. Somerset Maugham put on a special hat.

These routines may have started as practical measures—a candle for light, a hat to keep warm—but over time they developed into subliminal triggers. As Stephen King said, "The cumulative power of doing things the same way every day seems to be a way of saying to the mind: You're going to be dreaming soon." King's daily ritual begins when he sets a glass of water or tea on his desk, turns on the stereo, and swallows a vitamin pill.

If you cannot write at the same time each day (which many writers recommend) you can still close the door, turn off the phone, or put on some music. You can insert ear plugs, don a certain piece of clothing, or consciously breathe to center yourself. If you don't have a desk reserved for your work, you can make a ritual of clearing a space and setting up the things you need.

Many of us have difficulty with transitions, so it is important to recognize when you are shifting gears. In *The First Step*, Rabbi Zalman Schachter-Shalomi suggests a simple ritual to enhance your home life when you have an outside job. At the end of the work day, as you straighten your desk or pack your things, look around the office and consciously say good-bye. Then as you approach your house think of those already there—your mate, kids, cat, dog, even a favorite chair. By deliberately shifting your focus from work to home you can enjoy the experience of being there more fully.

Stephen King has a simple ritual for ending the writing day so he doesn't bring the horror of his work home to his family. He places a small plastic statue of Rocket J. Squirrel (of *Rocky & Bullwinkle* fame) on top of his work before closing the door.

Each of us has ritualized ways of getting up in the morning and going to bed at night, but we're usually unconscious of our routines. Try noticing how you brush your teeth and wash or shave your face. Are there habitual things you say to yourself in front of the mirror?

Imagine one of your characters performing his or her daily ablutions. Create a scene in which a ritual is interrupted by an important event, or a scene in which conversation takes place during a routine activity.

Is there a special way you prepare yourself before meeting someone you care about or receiving positive recognition? Try grooming yourself for an important date before sitting down at your desk and see how that affects your writing.

W. E. Reinka, author of *Dust of the Past* and *Blood on the Eagle's Feather*, suggests you alter some routine action to shake yourself out of a writing rut. If you always put your left shoe on first, start with your right shoe instead. If you always walk the dog around one particular block, head in a different direction. Eat something new for breakfast. A simple change can surprise your system and provide a burst of creative inspiration.

become the

Other

Gustave Flaubert so identified with the heroine of his most famous novel that he once remarked, *"Madame Bovary, c'est moi."* While describing the scene in which Bovary poisons herself, Flaubert became ill. "I had such a taste of arsenic in my mouth, I was so poisoned myself, that I had two attacks of indigestion, one after the other, very real attacks, for I vomited my dinner."

E. L. Doctorow has described novelists as people "who live in other people's skins."

Anne Sexton told the *Paris Review* that when she wrote a poem about a person, she became that person. "When I wrote about the farmer's wife, I lived in my mind in Illinois. When I had the illegitimate child, I nursed it—in my mind—and gave it back and traded life. . . . When I was Christ, I felt like Christ. My arms hurt, I desperately wanted to pull them off the Cross."

John LeCarre often gets inside a character's head by mentally putting on his clothes. When working on *The Tailor of Panama* he spent hours in a cafe, experiencing the anticipation, fear, and boredom one might feel waiting for a fellow spy. He noted the sounds, sights and subtle cues that caught his attention in this state.

Charles Dickens was known to be a terrific mimic capable of assuming any accent or persona. His daughter described him periodically jumping up from his desk to mime various facial expressions in the mirror before sitting back down to write. Like Dickens, playwright Angus Wilson acts out scenes and speaks dialogue when he is working.

When Allan Gurganus was writing *The Oldest Confederate Widow Tells All*, he was puzzled by his heroine Lucy Marston's use of the word *ain't*. So he took out a piece of paper and, titling it Why I Say Ain't, let Lucy explain for herself how, despite having been raised by a debutante mother, she came to speak colloquially. The resulting monologue evolved into a chapter in the book.

John Berendt, who wrote about actual people in *Midnight in the Garden of Good and Evil*, has a game he plays to strengthen his imagination. When he walks out of his apartment, he picks the first person he sees and imagines himself wearing that person's clothes for the rest of the day.

Patricia MacLachlan frequently practices being other people. "I even practice it when I'm watching stupid politics on television, and I'm thinking, 'How Can Pat Buchanan possibly say that we have to become isolationist?' Then I say, 'Here's how,' and I imagine I'm some poor person living near an immigrant area and my job is gone. My friends all laugh because I'm extremely opinionated, but every time they put somebody down I say, 'Wait a minute,' and they say, 'Oh, damn, here comes Patty trying to see the other person's point of view.'"

Allow yourself to become another person. Assume that character's walk, gestures, and accent. Order food as he or she would in a restaurant. Put on his or her clothes.

Try to convince a stranger of some truth in which your character believes. Not only will you experience the world through your character's eyes, you'll see how other people respond.

Like many writers, Newbery Award–winning author Patricia MacLachlan holds imaginary conversations with her characters. She often does this while driving in her car: "Nobody knows I'm having conversations," she says, "because they think I'm singing with the radio." You may find it helpful to let a character have a discussion directly with you on paper.

As Robert Stone once said, "If you really imagine your way into a character you find yourself in your dreams being that character, literally in your character's circumstances." So pay attention to your dreams to see if your characters play a role in them.

When I asked *San Francisco Chronicle* columnist Jon Carroll how he managed to come up with five columns a week, he recited these lines from Rudyard Kipling's *The Elephant's Child*:

> I have six humble serving men
> They taught me all I knew
> Their names are what
> and where and when
> and why and how and who.

ask a

Question

Kipling's serving men can help you through every stage of the writing process. They will unearth a story, construct a framework, and furnish it with vivid detail. They'll help you fix structural problems, demolish writing blocks, and navigate around creative obstacles.

Any one of the serving men can help you when you're feeling lost or unsure of your purpose. They keep nonfiction from becoming too abstract by eliciting anecdotes that bring your ideas to life. They help you make interesting choices that give your fictional characters depth and richness.

In his interview for *Writers Dreaming*, Allan Gurganus described how he used questions to build a world for Lucy Marston in *The Oldest Living Confederate Widow Tells All*: "You say, I will now create a ninety-nine-year-old woman. Where is she? She's in a charity rest home. [*Why?*] She doesn't have any money left. [*Why?*] She gave it all away. *Who* does she see in the course of a day? She sees the people who help her. *Who* are they? There's a nurse . . . And *how* do we make the nurse particular? Well, he's gay . . . and he wears a T-shirt that says Disco Ain't Dead Yet and he makes quilts, and he does massages for old people and he does their hair. . . ."

Try building a character now, using Kipling's serving men as guides. Begin with simple questions—Who is my protagonist? When and where does he or she live? What are this person's passions? Deficiencies? How does he begin each day? What is a typical breakfast? Lunch? Where does she spend her leisure time? Let your character have a few strong traits—some specific needs, desires, or fears. Make your choices interesting, but don't try to be too outrageous. Your characters will acquire uniqueness from the accumulation of specific detail. Who are this character's allies? Enemies? What crisis is he or she about to face? When and where will it happen?

At several writers' conferences I've heard editors complain about stories in which, by the end of the first paragraph, they're still wondering who it is that's talking. A reader shouldn't have to guess if the speaker is male or female, young or old, and so on. Review the piece you're working on to be certain you have established the who, what, where, and when of your story, so that a stranger can see what you are seeing.

If you are looking for a story idea, Mary Higgens Clark recommends the magic question *What if?* She found inspiration for *Loves Music, Loves to Dance* when, after perusing the ads in a local paper, she asked herself, "What if a serial killer were to use the personals to find his victims?" Robert Harris wrote *Fatherland* and Phillip K. Dick wrote *The Man in the High Castle* after asking themselves, "What if Germany had won World War II?" Elizabeth Berg wrote *Talk Before Sleep* to imagine what she and her best friend might have discussed if the friend had voiced her feelings as she battled a fatal cancer.

Make a list of "what if" questions and then choose one to play with. What if the earth went out of orbit? What if money ceased to have value? What if you had been born a female in Iran? Use "what if" to help extricate a character from a sticky situation. What if he were to jump out the window? You might follow the question with "Where would he land? What bones would he break?"

Create a deck of question cards to use whenever you feel stuck. Print one question on each of seven blank cards—you should have six serving men cards and one that reads "What if?" (You might make an eighth card that reads "Why not?") Next time you pull a "when" card, it may prompt you to ask, "At what time of day is this scene taking place?" Or "When did the actual turning point occur?" The "why" card may remind you to illustrate a character's motivation or prompt you to explain some phenomenon you've been describing.

Instead of pulling different question cards, try staying with one for as long as you can. Let each repetition take you deeper and deeper. For instance, keep asking, "Where?" You'll find that your imagery becomes more specific: Where did the crime occur? On the campus. Where? In Doe Library. Where? In the women's restroom. Where? By the paper towel dispenser. Where? Wedged between the two sinks. To pinpoint the time of the crime, repeatedly ask yourself "When?" To flesh out the details, ask "How?"

You might want to create a large deck of questions cards, with ten longer questions per serving man. One of the "what" cards could say, "What happened?" Another might say, "What *will* happen?" Another, "What changed? Write generic questions that will prompt you to examine consequences, causes, needs, assumptions, power relationships, and dangers. Some cards may ask about the past; some, the present; some, the future. You can pull a question card at random or scan the deck and choose the one that seems most appropriate at a given time.

inertia or indifference. If you're feeling stuck, list twenty questions you might want to explore or five magazines you could query. If you're planning to write a book, start with a list of chapter titles. This could trigger a new phase of productive writing.

Stretch your imagination by choosing a large, specific number (10, 25, 52, 100) of ideas to generate. If you have told yourself you need twenty-five conflicts from which to choose, do not stop at twenty-three or twenty-four. An extra push to meet your quota can force a great idea to surface.

An essential element in Ira Progoff's Intensive Journal Workshop is the creation of what he calls logs. To write about a period in your life, first list people important to you at that time. Make sure to include family, friends, and influential teachers, as well as employees, coworkers, and bosses. Also list the newsmakers—politicians, religious leaders, film stars—who impacted your psyche. Then list all the things you were involved in during this period—jobs, hobbies, volunteer activities. List everything you were concerned about—family troubles, money worries, finding purpose. In the course of creating these logs, you will awaken old memories and create a richer picture of that time.

variations

If you have pulled the "Make a List" card before, you can always go to an earlier list, choose one item, and write about it.

Create a box of memories for a friend. Novelist Julie Winokur and her husband received such a box from the woman who baby-sat their children. The baby-sitter asked them each separately to share with her ten memories from a ten-year period in each of their lives. She jotted each memory on a notecard and placed it in the box. Winokur says, "Each card contains an entire story which can now be developed into a piece of writing or strung together as definitive events in two people's lives."

build a

History

Ken Follett had written ten moderately successful novels when agent/editor Al Zuckerman pointed out a problem in Follett's work: "None of these characters has a past." The characters were flat, came from nowhere, and had no existence off the page. Heeding Zuckerman's advice, Follett spent time getting to know the characters for his eleventh novel. He imagined where they'd grown up, how they'd been educated, where they'd been employed—everything that had happened to them up to the moment the story began. Though much of this information never appeared in *The Eye of the Needle,* it helped Follett develop the complex characters that made the book an international best-seller.

"You can't start with how people look and speak and behave and come to know how they feel," said Eudora Welty. "You must know exactly what's in their hearts and minds *before* they ever set visible foot on the stage. You must know all, then not tell it all, or not tell too much at once."

Many writers create elaborate dossiers for their characters. They know not only how they appear, but how they evolved into their present selves. They know their strengths and weaknesses, their triumphs and traumas, their habits and tics. They can describe a character's typical work day and average Saturday night. They know a character's favorite music, mode of transport, and breakfast food, plus all their health, money, and relationship issues.

Judith Krantz has a file for every character she creates. When she has a thought about one of them, she puts it on a piece of paper and tucks it in the appropriate folder. She also tears pictures of people, clothes, and homes from magazines and throws them into each character's file.

Sometimes a piece of imagined history can become a whole new story. When Patricia MacLachlan was writing *Sarah, Plain and Tall,* she sensed that the widower Jacob was a man of sadness even before his first wife died. Researching prairie literature, MacLachlan discovered that many men deserted their families during difficult times, and realized that Jacob's sadness was probably the result of such an abandonment. This back story never appeared in *Sarah, Plain and Tall,* but, when faced with the demand for sequels and prequels, MacLachlan used it as the basis for another book.

You want to know not only the history and habits of your characters, but also the history of the places, ideas, and institutions about which you write. When Rand and Robyn Miller wanted to invent a computer game where players didn't have to kill to win, they decided to create a secret world for people to explore. To keep players interested they needed some mystery, so they gave their world an elaborate history. Though the game was nonlinear, the Millers needed some sort of internal logic to guide their invention. So they made up a story about an island ruled by feuding brothers. From this they generated clues which players could uncover in letters, maps, and journals while wandering through the world. When Myst became the best-selling computer game in history and Hyperion Publishers approached the Miller brothers about a companion book, they already had plenty of material from which to create it.

If you are working on a piece of fiction, create a background file on one of your characters today. You might try Ira Progroff's Stepping Stones technique–imagine the twelve most significant events in the character's life starting with birth and ending with the present moment.

Pulitzer Prize–winning author Edward Humes recommends visiting the local historical society where your piece is set so that you can sprinkle tidbits of history throughout the story. The details of Savannah history woven through John Berendt's *Midnight in the Garden of Good and Evil* added color and richness to the story.

Author Gillian Roberts advises mystery writers to give their protagonists a number of skills they may not seem to need right away. These skills can be useful if a book becomes a series. Roberts laments that she didn't give her heroine Amanda Pepper a black belt in karate or fluency in a foreign language, as these would have come in handy in later books. It was too late to introduce them once the first book was published. Roberts also sometimes regrets having made Amanda a school teacher because, between 8 A.M. and 4 P.M., the only bodies she can discover have to be on school grounds (and there are only so many times one can find a corpse in the auditorium). Give your hero or heroine extra skills and build flexibility into the lives of your characters right from the start.

If you are not in the midst of a project now, pick someone off the street and imagine his or her history. How many children, if any, does this person have? Where does he or she work? Has there been a major crisis in this person's life? Look for clues in your subject's dress, location, and demeanor. To get beyond the obvious choices, develop several different scenarios.

Allan Gurganus *(The Oldest Living Confederate Widow Tells All)* says, "When I am doing it right, I know not only what is in my characters' wallets . . . but I could tell you what the great-grandmother's wallet was like and–generationally, classwise, historically–the matrix that this person came from." You might not want to go back three generations, but it could prove useful to try.

You can interpret character to mean a place, invention, or institution. Imagine the people who occupied a house over several generations. Picture the dramas that occurred in various rooms. What was the neighborhood like when the house was first built?

Trace the history of a corporation—what was the original need the founder set out to fill? How did the company grow? What became of the early players? Who were the competitors, the customers, the first investors?

Pick an object—a can opener, a doorknob, a football—and imagine its history. Where was it made? How did it get here? Who has it belonged to? What adventures did it experience? Write a brief history of the object in either the first or third person.

I recently tried an exercise introduced to me by Sue Bender, author of *Plain and Simple* and *Everyday Sacred*. For many months, Sue had struggled to draw a perfect pear. Frustrated, she turned to an artist friend who suggested that Sue was looking at the pear too hard. The woman told her to *squint*, and then draw what she observed. When she did, her drawing improved immeasurably.

I decided to try Sue's exercise one day when I was sitting on a beach looking

Squint

across Monterey Bay. It is a view people travel thousands of miles to see, but I found myself unable to enjoy it. So I squinted. Suddenly I saw all sorts of things I hadn't noticed before. With my eyes scrunched together, I saw how the masts of nearby sailboats were reflected in the water where they created a pattern of parallel lines. I saw that motif echoed by the poles holding up a nearby pier. And I noticed for the first time the glimmering patterns that sunlight cast upon the water. As I became aware of the shadows created by a passing couple, I felt a deep sense of happiness. Looked at directly, the scene had been too familiar, too much like a postcard or a vacation brochure. Squinting helped me see the scene without expectations.

Take some time right now to squint. Scrunch up your eyes and notice the verticals and horizontals of your world. Notice how light reflects off various surfaces. Notice the shapes and patterns you've taken for granted. Record what you see and anything your sight inspires. Start by simply writing down random words and phrases. Dorothy Wall suggests you apply your words to the paper as an impressionist dabs paint on a canvas. You need not make sentences. You don't even have to make sense.

If you are working on a piece set in a familiar location, revisit that setting and squint. You will discover new aspects of that world you never expected. You might stumble onto a metaphor. You might find yourself automatically imagining one or more characters appearing on the scene, moving about the space, touching objects, interacting. Spend a few minutes squinting at just one object or one spot, then begin to write. Write for ten minutes. Again, you can simply put down random words and impressions. Or you might find a concrete scene that you can sketch out on the page.

Look at your world through a mirror. Choose one of the mirrors in your house, stand off to the side so that you cannot see yourself, and look at the scene reflected in the glass. If the mirror is on a door or cabinet, slowly swing the door and notice all that the mirror reveals. You may want to imagine a person in the scene or simply describe the planes and surfaces that you see from this new perspective.

Carry a small mirror with you as you travel through your day. Visit places that relate to what you are writing. See what appears behind you as you walk or drive or sit.

Roll up a piece of paper and create a pirate's looking glass. Swivel your head while looking through the porthole you've created. Take imaginary snapshots. Move your looking glass close to a wall or a household appliance. By limiting your field of vision, you take familiar objects out of context and see in terms of shape and form.

Sometimes, when you think you haven't got any ideas, you actually have too many. Your mind may feel blank because it's clogged with thoughts all caught in a jumble. You need to construct a channel through which your ideas can flow. Like water through a garden hose, the narrower the opening through which you pass a stream of thought, the more powerful the output.

Set limits—time limits, page limits, rules of rhyme or meter. Restrict your word

Set Limits

count, your subject matter, or the time frame of your story to help you write more effectively.

If you think a project is going to eat up all your time, you may resist it for fear of depriving yourself of other pleasures. If you think you have all the time in the world you may never get started. Tell yourself that you will spend only so much time on your writing each day. The rest of your time is reserved for pleasure, friends, or family.

Novelist Graham Greene made himself write exactly 500 words per day. As soon as he reached that number he would stop, no matter when this occurred or where he was in his story. He restricted his output so he could have a life to write about. He made himself do 500 words so he could have a career.

Yoruba Priestess Luisah Teish wrote *Jambalaya* and *Carnival of the Spirits* with the help of a kitchen timer she called Minerva. Recognizing that she could never get anything done in the daytime—what with a family, the telephone, and a busy consulting practice—she retreated to her office at night after everyone else had settled down. She set the timer for fifty minutes and didn't stop writing until the bell rang. Then she would let herself have something to eat.

Christina Buchmann, author of *Out of the Garden*, used an egg timer to help her complete her doctoral thesis. She found the ticking a comforting sound. Whatever she could accomplish in the thirty to sixty minutes she'd allot herself would have to suffice. "It was safe to concentrate really hard because I knew the work was not going to take over my life, not going to be so overwhelming I wouldn't be able to get out of it."

If you're just starting on a project, it may be futile to tell yourself you must write all weekend or put in three hours every day. Start small. Tell yourself you will write for fifteen minutes on one specific topic today. And let that be enough. Even if you write nothing brilliant in those fifteen minutes, you will have accomplished what you set out to do. And you may find the process so productive that you will be happy to risk another quarter-hour tomorrow.

It is very difficult for most people to work without a deadline. If you don't already have one, join or form a group that meets every week so that you'll be forced to produce new material. Even if you only work a few frantic hours the day before the meeting, you will be getting something done.

Otherwise, find a contest you can enter—this will not only give you a time limit, but will provide restrictions as to length and content. Edna St. Vincent Millay, E. B. White, Ring Lardner, and F. Scott Fitzgerald all began writing to win competitions sponsored by the St. Nicholas League.

Writing to specification helps you crystallize your thoughts. You may be brimming over with feelings but, unless you find a container to hold them, they can be lost. Pick a form that you can work in and let the rules of that tradition define your parameters.

If you want to write for children, remember that the typical children's picture book is only thirty-two pages long. The necessity of filling, but not exceeding, that number will force you to be more creative. If you want to work in magazines, pick a periodical in which you'd like to be published and make your work fit their standard format.

Robert Frost once said, "Writing free verse is like playing tennis without a net." Express your feelings about love or money within the restrictions of the sonnet form. Or write a simple haiku. If you want to create a screenplay, honor the traditional three act structure laid out in any how-to-write-a-screenplay book. If you want to write for theater, try doing a one-act play. Restrict yourself to Aristotle's unities—make the whole story happen in one place on one day.

Limit what it is you're going to write about today. You may want to do one character sketch or set up a particular scene. You may need to create an outline or write one conversation. Choosing just one task will narrow your focus and improve your concentration.

conduct an

Interview

Often, in the course of a writing project, you need information that only another person can provide. You may need to know how some piece of equipment works, what happens during a liver transplant, or how some town in Provence smells in the spring. You may need statistics that have not yet been published or a clear explanation of low-temperature physics.

When Edgar Award–winning author Julie Smith was writing her first mystery novel, she needed a suitable weapon with which to kill a victim who plays tennis. Looking up country clubs in the yellow pages, she found a tennis pro to give her advice. He asked the height and weight of the victim and then recommended a Wilson 2000, instructing Smith to make sure the killer turned the racket on its side.

If you're trying to develop a character, talking to someone with a similar profile may trigger anecdotes, phrases, or gestures you can use.

When writing a memoir, it is often useful to talk to relatives, teachers, and friends—they'll help you fill in a memory or provide a different version of some situation.

Using the telephone for interviewing allows you to take notes without having to maintain eye contact and allows interviewees to reveal themselves without the discomfort of being seen. You can hook a tape recorder up to the phone with an inexpensive gadget available at any Radio Shack, but be sure to tell your subject that he or she is being taped.

When you first call for an interview, recognize that this may not be the best time to talk and ask for an appointment. On the other hand, your subject may say, "Let's do it now," so be prepared. Make sure you are familiar with your subject's work, as well as any articles that have been written about him or her. Knowing plenty of background information will help you steer the conversation.

If you can only get through to a receptionist or secretary, treat this person as an ally. Enlist his or her help in getting the information you need. I became good friends with Stephen King's assistant over the course of the year that I pursued an interview with him. After I had explained why I needed the interview, she told me the best approach to take: "Write a letter," she said, "but keep it short!" Each of my four letters was sent to King's assistant with a note requesting that she place it on King's desk when she thought he'd be most receptive. The day he finally consented to talk, she was as excited as I was.

Prepare a list of questions, but don't feel obliged to ask them all. You are better off probing one question deeply than covering a number superficially. Listen to each answer and let it inspire your next question. Follow up with "Why?" Or "What do you mean?" Or "Could you give me an example?"

Keep the tape recorder running after you've formally wrapped up an interview. Some of the best material comes out when your subject assumes you're through.

Terry Gross, host of the national radio program *Fresh Air,* often asks how a subject's life or views were changed by some event. She establishes powerful intimacy with her guests by starting out with safe questions and only asking charged, highly personal ones after achieving rapport with them. She gives her subjects permission not to answer questions that make them uncomfortable. Feeling safe, they reveal far more to her than they would to other interviewers.

Never assume that people do not want to talk to you. Private investigator Melody Ermachild, author of *Altars in the Street*, taught me that you can get anyone to talk if you simply keep quiet and listen. People will share information that could land them in jail simply because they want their side of a story heard.

To overcome resistance, validate the person's experience. When I began an interview for *Writers Dreaming*, an author would sometimes insist that he or she never remembered dreams. I responded with, "Most people tell me that, but I'll bet you can remember a childhood dream." I'd then list the ones most people told me— falling, flying, being chased. The simple reassurance that they were not alone, coupled with gentle prompting, almost always produced results.

With some authors, I had to invoke the competitive spirit. "Well, John Barth told me a dream about . . ." helped William Styron open up. Recognizing that I had interviewed someone of Barth's stature, and not wanting to be outdone, he told me of the dream that led to *Sophie's Choice*.

When working in market research—I was the woman with a clipboard in the shopping mall asking strangers their opinions on laundry detergents and soft drinks—I learned several probing techniques from my boss, Susan Taylor. My favorite is called What Else.

Taylor said that most people don't really know what they think or feel the first time they are asked a question. They respond with clichés or superficial answers. Often people resist telling all because the truth seems too stupid, obvious, or naughty to share with another person. A good interviewer establishes trust by listening attentively and, knowing that the truth may take time to surface, asks "What else?" to help the subject dig deeper. "What else?" is a lovely nonthreatening prompt that conveys the message "Of course there is more."

It is more important to probe one or two questions deeply than to cover ten superficially. Another of Taylor's techniques involves repeating the last word said by the other person. Let's say you are asking a rather laconic writer about his source of inspiration and you begin with the rather uninspiring question "Where do you get your ideas?" He answers glibly, "From TV."

TV?
Yeah, I watch crime shows.
Crime shows?
Well, I like old *Dragnet* episodes.
Dragnet shows?
Yeah, and *Untouchables* reruns.
Anything else?
Well I like cartoons a lot.
Cartoons?
Yeah, *Rocky and Bullwinkle*.
Rocky and Bullwinkle?
Yeah, I love Natasha.
What is it you like about Natasha?
Her mouth.
What about her mouth?
She has cruel lips.
Cruel lips?
Yeah, they remind me of my third grade teacher.

Interview yourself. Choose an issue you'd like to explore or a problem that needs solving and capture it on paper in question form. For fiction you might ask, "How can my hero escape?" Or "Where should the first encounter occur?" Or "When is the secret best revealed?" Write down your answer and then write "What else?" Answer again, and repeat the exercise to let more answers emerge. This technique will take you deeper and deeper in or further and further out.

When building a character, constructing a plot, or solving a writing problem, don't settle for the first thought that pops into your mind. If you're trying to define your heroine's problem, don't assume your initial thought is the best one. Ask, "What else could her problem be?" Or "What else could she do in this situation?"

If you are working in nonfiction, probe for the less-than-obvious cause. You might ask, "What is the reason that children can't learn? What is the secret to baking great bread? What are the lessons to be learned from this story?" Always follow up with What else? What else? What else?

Instruments

For years my family badgered my father to write down his memories. We wanted to know where he came from and how he became who he was. But as much as he wanted to do so, something always got in the way. Finally my sister convinced him to use a tape recorder and he set about capturing his thoughts.

It turns out that several great authors dictated their work. Fydor Dostoevsky used a stenographer (who later became his second wife) to create *The Gambler* and *Crime and Punishment*. Winston Churchill dictated his speeches, essays, and correspondence, and won a Nobel Prize in literature for work composed aloud. Isak Dinesen would never have written *Out of Africa* had a publisher not sent her a secretary to whom she could speak her memoirs. James Thurber, Eugene Ionesco, and Henry James all used dictation when age or infirmity made writing difficult.

My dad hired a woman to type up his taped reminiscences, and out of the rambling transcript he extracted some wonderful anecdotes. Relieved to discover he had stories worth sharing, he enrolled in a memoir class where, with concrete assignments, set deadlines, and a captive audience to entertain, his writing soon took off.

The tape recorder has been a useful catalyst, but to write well my dad needed to switch instruments. His initial, unsuccessful attempts at writing had been on a computer–but the machine made everything too official, too permanent. In class, he learned that his thoughts flowed more easily and coherently through a pen. Still, a computer was an excellent tool for revising because he automatically made improvements while retyping assignments for his class.

Monologuist Spalding Gray prefers handwriting, describing it as an extension of his musculature, "the closest thing I can get to breath." Gray composes on paper, corrects in red pen, and then reads his work rapidly into a tape recorder. As he reads, he skips, adds, and replaces words, so that another round of editing occurs even before the tapes are transcribed.

It may seem surprising how many authors still write by hand, but William Styron, Clive Barker, John Barth, Gore Vidal, Norman Mailer, and Joyce Carol Oates all use pen and paper for part of the writing process.

Today, if you normally work on a computer, try writing by hand. If you normally use a pen or pencil, type. Or, write with a crayon, a magic marker, a calligraphy pen. Imagine how one of your characters might form words on paper, and adopt his or her style of writing. Switch to cursive script or bold block letters. Write with your nondominant hand.

Critic William Gass dramatically and deliberately changed his handwriting when he was in college. For years afterwards he wrote in a hand he described as very Germanic and stiff. "That change of script was a response to my family situation," he told the *Paris Review*. "I fled an emotional problem and hid myself behind a wall of arbitrary formality. Nevertheless, I think that if I eventually write anything which has any enduring merit, it will be in part because of that odd alteration."

Experiment with your mode of writing. This can be an excellent way of unlocking your inhibitions as well as a way to improve your sense of self as a writer.

When T. S. Eliot was in the midst of a dry period he began writing poems in French. "I think that when I was writing in French I didn't take the poems so seriously, and that, not taking them seriously, I wasn't worried about not being able to write."

Polish-born authors Joseph Conrad and Jerzy Kosinski both found writing in English liberating and became literary masters only in this second language.

I often sing songs to my dog in Spanish since the few words I know—corazon, amor, and pimienta (which means "pepper," her name)—are much more conducive to expressions of affection than the familiar *heart* and *love*.

On the other hand, you may find that you can express certain emotions more effectively in your native tongue. Isabel Allende continues to write in Spanish even though she has lived in America for years.

Sandra Boynton, creator of the famous "Hippo Birdie Two Ewes" birthday card, as well as a line of other cards, cups, and calendars, did a whole album of "Pigorian" chants combining the bits of Latin she remembered from high school with pig latin.

Try writing in a different language or create a character with an interesting accent. You may find this loosens your writing and takes you into uncharted territory.

The way a character moves through space can tell you more about him than the statistics on his driver's license or the details of his resume. The tapping foot, the wandering eye, and the scratching finger all provide clues into a person's internal life.

Pulitzer Prize–winning author E. Annie Proulx began *The Shipping News* by describing her hero's habit of covering his chin with his hand. Within a few paragraphs we understand why: the man has a

watch for
Gesture

large lantern jaw and is terribly shy because of it. The gesture, repeated at critical moments, helps us remember the man's vulnerability as his character evolves through the course of the book.

John LeCarre is a master at depicting the subtle gesture that helps conjure a complex human being. In *The Secret Pilgrim*, the Polish torturer Colonel Jerzy looks his most forlorn just before he is about to hurt his victim. In the final moments before he strikes a blow, he rubs his hand sadly across his rich, full mouth. In one crucial scene we see Ned, the narrator-victim, anticipating an attack as his assailant executes the telltale movement: "He passed the back of his hand across his lips, a thing he sometimes did before he hit me." But then, instead of hitting Ned, the colonel offers an unusual confession. LeCarre has created suspense using gesture to set up and confound the reader's expectation.

Take time to focus on the body language of the people around you. Pick one person to study, focusing on hands, face, posture, feet. Notice fingers, shoulders, eyebrows, mouth. Where does he carry his center of gravity? What animal image does she evoke? How?

Spend time watching a number of people engaged in the same activity, like talking on the telephone. The airport is a terrific place to watch several people on the phone at once. Notice the different ways people tilt their heads, handle their receivers, position their feet. What kind of facial expressions do they exhibit? What clues do they give about the nature of their calls? Or their emotions? Carry your notebook or some index cards to jot down what you observe. Later, try mimicking the different postures and imagine what it might feel like to be each of these people.

Acting teacher F. Jo Mohrbach tells her students that it is far easier to re-create an emotion when the actor is occupied in action than when he is simply emoting on stage. She points out how Bette Davis always had something in her hand—a cigarette, a cup of coffee—so that her character's feelings were communicated through physical action.

Mohrbach has her acting students fold laundry, chop wood, or wash dishes when delivering a powerful speech. Thus her actors have more tools with which to express feelings and are not forced to rely on facial expressions.

Take a scene you have written and give your characters a new activity to engage in as they relate to one another. Have them cooking or shopping or changing a tire and see how this improves the dialogue. Or create a whole new scene by engaging several characters in a routine activity and letting the dialogue develop.

Next time you are on public transportation or stuck in a traffic jam, observe the people around you. Where are their eyes focused?

How are their hands occupied? What nonverbal clues are they offering as to their destinations?

Watch people walking down a street. Do some lead with their heads while others lead with bellies or feet? Notice the various gaits and speeds. Try smiling at various strangers and observe their reactions.

Watch a group of people eating a meal together. Notice the different ways that they handle silverware, use a napkin, and chew. Pay attention to posture, gestures, and signs of how they relate to one another. Then write a scene in which two people argue over breakfast. Punctuate your dialogue with specific movements.

variations

Explore the symbolic content of a personal habit—your own or someone else's. Consider the unconscious messages the habit may convey. For instance, I have a friend who splits her hair. Watching her do it evokes images of monkeys searching for lice and biblical widows rending their hair in grief. I wonder how the phrase *splitting hairs* relates to this practice. Watching my friend brings back memories from the sixth grade, sitting cross-legged on the floor of the gymnasium and working to effect the perfect glossy, straight-haired look then in fashion.

Write about your earliest memory involving a personal habit. Describe the most dramatic incident involving this habit—the time someone made fun of you for it or the day you finally quit doing it. Incorporate such an incident into your fiction. Let it inspire an essay or a chapter in your memoirs.

locate the Fear

According to Dr. Robert Maurer, professor of psychology at UCLA, fear lies at the center of all great fiction. Every character is afraid of something—of loss, of failure, of success, of being unmasked—and drama is to be found in how each character copes with his or her fears. While one character might be afraid of growing old alone, another might be afraid that some secret of his past will be revealed, and another might harbor the fear that she will turn out just like her mother.

In order to give your characters depth and your stories dramatic tension, you must determine what your characters fear and how they deal with it.

Think about someone you know or someone you are currently writing about. You can pick a person you see on the street or a character you are creating. What is this person afraid of? Is it fear of being poor or growing fat? Is it fear of being hurt or of hurting another person? Make a list of ten or fifteen things which a character might be afraid of. If you are writing mysteries or horror, the dangers your characters face might be far more concrete (death, incarceration, dismemberment) than in a literary novel, but you should also be sure that they have ordinary human fears (poverty, loneliness, loss of a loved one).

Think about the ways your characters deal with their fears. Do they face them head on or run away? Do they drown themselves in alcohol or try to forget through sex? Do they invite trouble into their lives, or create safe but dull existences?

Next time you go to the movies or rent a video, explore the fears that motivate each of the characters. Look at how each person manifests or disguises those fears.

Try sketching a short two-person scene in which the fears and needs of one character are at odds with the fears and needs of another character—in fact, the fears of one may exacerbate those of the other. For example, one person's fear of commitment triggers the other's fear of abandonment. Or one person's fear of being conned comes up against the other's fear of being misunderstood. Place your two characters in a setting in which they are doing something physical while carrying on a conversation that illustrates the clash. The physical activity will help you demonstrate the dynamics without having to resort to obvious dialogue. While moving a heavy piece of furniture, for example, a couple may argue about how to maneuver around a corner or who is to walk backwards.

Your own fears are a valuable source of material. Mystery writer Julie Smith was looking for a new book idea when she realized she needed a worthy adversary for her heroine, Skip Langdon. She wanted a villain as evil as Arthur Conan Doyle's Moriarty or Thomas Harris's Hanibal Lector. She wanted the devil incarnate. Looking back on her past, she remembered interviewing the Reverend Jim Jones, a man who later caused the death of more than 900 people at Jonestown. During their initial meeting, Jones seemed to know things about Smith that no one else could have known. Only later did she discover that he had people go through her garbage and watch her house to get the information he seemed to possess so miraculously. Jones had terrified Smith, and she used this encounter to create the villain in *The Kindness of Strangers*.

Think of someone in your past who has evoked fear in you or in others. Describe what qualities made this person so terrifying. Detail some of the techniques he or she used to intimidate, insinuate, or manipulate. Create a scene in which you or one of your characters encounters such a person and prevails.

Sue Grafton, creator of the alphabet mystery series (*A Is for Alibi*, *B Is for Burglar*, etc.) says that, because she sits in front of her computer all day, she has little actual experience of terror. So she looks to her dreams. When she wakes up from a nightmare she catalogs her physical sensations—sweaty palms, thumping heart—and applies them to her heroine, Kinsey Milhone, when she encounters danger.

Think back to a terrifying moment in your life—a car accident, a walk down an unlit street, a situation in which you were almost caught doing something wrong—and describe the physical sensations you experienced. Write down the thoughts that went through your head at the time. Record any delayed reactions you had as well.

Children's book author Maurice Sendak uses the fears of childhood as the basis for much of his writing. He says the monsters of *Where the Wild Things Are* are really the old Jewish relatives who delighted in pinching his cheeks and declaring their desire to "eat him up" when he was a child. In Yiddish, unruly children are often referred to as *vilde chayas*, which means "wild animals."

Take a few minutes to think about something that terrified you when you were little. Write from a child's point of view.

"What I love is when totally disparate facts come together," John Cheever told the *Paris Review*. He was describing how a story evolved as he sat in a cafe reading a letter from home. He was reading about a married neighbor who was due to appear in a nude review, when he overheard a woman scolding her children: "If you don't do thus and so before mummy counts to three . . ." Just then a leaf fell, reminding him of winter and the fact that his wife had left him.

combine

Elements

When he combined these elements, a story emerged.

Novelist Elizabeth Berg has said that combining elements is one of her favorite techniques. For years she carried around three disparate ideas hoping to use each in a story. There was a game she liked to play with license plates (LIN232 could be Love Is Now or Lou Is Nothing). There was also the term *white dwarf,* which she'd heard described an imploded star. And there was something she'd read about a bird, the grackle, that pecked other birds to death. Berg wove all three elements into one conversation in which a man realizes that his wife has been unfaithful. The story, originally titled White Dwarf, was published in *Redbook* under the name "Big Getaway."

Jane Smiley says that fiction comes out of the juxtaposition of elements. "You're not just relating something that happened. You're imagining how two things would fit together." I had phoned Smiley for advice on creating a story from a newspaper article. She said it was far better to combine elements from two different stories than to try to fictionalize just one. Rather than writing about a man in a homeless shelter or a man in an avalanche, she suggested I create a relationship between the two and see what emerged.

If you already have a couple of loose ideas waiting for a story, try putting them together into one piece. Or make a list of story ideas to mix and match at random.

Cut paper into fifty phrase-sized strips. On each one write a different noun, verb, or adjective. Include people, places, activities, and seasons. Jot down any stray phrases you'd like to use. Stir the pile of strips around, pull three, and work them into a story or essay. If you are in the midst of a writing project, pull one piece of paper and find a way to incorporate its contents into your work.

This exercise can shift your focus from worrying about how well you write to solving a concrete problem. In the process, you may uncover an issue that excites you. And you will now have a fresh vehicle with which to explore that theme.

Another way to enrich your work is by making various characters connect. Neil Simon was working on an early draft of *Come Blow Your Horn* when writer Billy Friedberg pointed out the lack of interaction between several characters. He suggested that Simon write all the characters' names in a circle and draw a line between them whenever two people interact. Simon created new scenes to make sure that all the lines crisscrossed and, in so doing, constructed a far better play.

W. H. Auden combines a technical problem—like meter, diction, or form—with a theme to create a poem. "The theme looks for the right form, the form looks for the right theme. When the two come together I am able to start writing."

Give yourself the challenge of combining an idea or activity with an unlikely structure—write a sonnet about washing dishes or a country western song about learning Spanish. The juxtaposition of elements will free your mind to work in unexpected ways.

Since you have pulled the "Combine Elements," card you may want to take this opportunity to pull two more cards from the deck and see how you can combine them. How would you combine "Take a Walk" with "Study a Photograph"? You might take a camera on your walk. Or imagine walking into the scene of a photograph. You might take pictures of people walking or walk to a photo gallery. Make a list of possiblities and then choose one to do.

"The fiction that artistic labor happens in isolation, and that artistic accomplishment is exclusively the provenance of individual talents is . . . in my case at least, repudiated by the facts," wrote Pulitzer Prize–winning playwright Tony Kushner. Without the input of the two dozen people who contributed to his epic *Angels in America*, Kushner says "the plays would have been entirely different—would, in fact, have never come to be."

The myth of the individual keeps many

Get Help

of us struggling in isolation, believing we must do it all alone.

Take a look at the acknowledgments in any number of successful books, and you'll see that most writers have people "without whom this book would not have been possible." They give thanks to people like the neighbor who took the kids for two hours or the partner who took up the slack at the office so a project could get done.

"Ask a favor, make a friend" is one of my father's favorite sayings. People love to be useful because it gives them a feeling of worth. Do not be afraid to ask someone for help. You can always return the favor by being a good listener, giving encouragement, or helping in some other way.

Many writers have loved ones who have served as first readers: Elmore Leonard had his wife; Isabel Allende, her mother; Amy Tan, her writers' group. Judith Krantz consults her husband when she feels stuck. She lays out a number of options, they discuss possible solutions, and then she picks the one she likes best. Anne Sexton once said that when she was working on a poem she'd call Maxine Kumin "every other line."

I might never have created *Writers Dreaming* had I not hired Dorothy Wall as a writing consultant. She helped me clarify my ideas and forced me to be specific when I wrote in generalities. She provided deadlines and encouraged me to keep on writing.

You might ask another writer to recommend a good consultant or peruse the ads in writers' magazines. Interview potential editors to find out how they work. Make sure that you do not seek help from people who haven't got your best interests in mind. You have your own strengths and weaknesses and are not meant to write in some-one else's style. Look for someone who is happy to help you clarify *your* vision and achieve *your* goals.

Even the great T. S. Eliot was helped by Ezra Pound, who edited *The Wasteland* down from a much longer piece. "He was a mar-velous critic," said Eliot, "because he didn't try to turn you into an imitation of himself. He tried to see what you were trying to do."

Jane Smiley cautions against reading your work to others in hopes of finding approval: "If they have an enthusiastic reaction, rather than sending you back to the typewriter, my experience is that it makes you feel like you've already accomplished your goals. And if they have even the slightest doubtful or negative reaction, then that takes the wind out of your sails."

I stopped writing for almost ten years after a "friend" told me my work was self-indulgent. Since he couldn't show me how to make the work more accessible, the only result of this feedback was a deep sense of shame. My mistake was in showing raw material to someone who did not have the skills or time to help me shape the work.

Development trainer Michael Mercil recommends that you be very specific when you ask for feedback. Don't ask, "Do you think this is good or not?" Ask a question the person can answer: "Is it clear what I am saying in this paragraph? What do you think is being said? Does this character elicit your sympathy? And if not, why not?" Ask, "Where did I lose your attention?" Or "Where was the energy strongest for you?"

Maybe now is a good time for you to take a class or join a writers group. Before you join, though, find out how the group is structured. See what kind of recommendations the class or group has. Not all situations will be right for you, so try to attend a session first to observe the quality of feedback. You probably don't want a group in which people take pleasure in ripping others' work apart. You deserve an experience that encourages you to grow in your most natural direction.

You might put an ad in a local paper or check the Internet, including my site (www.observationdeck.com), for people who want to start a writers' group. A group can provide tremendous support, and you'll have the opportunity to learn from the other participants.

The help you need right now may be very simple: someone to make you mail off a submission, a friend who will call each day to make sure that you are writing, or a gift from your spouse of an hour of privacy three evenings a week. Decide what you really need, and develop a strategy for getting it.

Although confidence is an important key to becoming a successful writer, most of us have a terrible time finding it. We wonder why anyone would be interested in what we have to say; we torture ourselves about the skills we lack; we fear we will never have enough drive, discipline, or imagination.

So what can you do when you're struggling? Pretend you are successful. Act like you are an accomplished author or are well on your way to becoming one. Sit up tall.

act

Successful

Relax your face. Assume the body language of an artist engaged in important work. By adjusting your posture you improve your circulation and invigorate your mind.

As you write, imagine friends and strangers enjoying your work. You might even write a stellar review of your work and pull it out whenever your confidence wanes. Mark Salzman, author of *Iron and Silk*, *The Soloist*, and *The Laughing Buddha*, used this strategy to transform his attitude toward the cello. When he practiced he pretended he was in front of a large audience at the Hollywood Bowl. Each note, no matter how badly played, brought murmurs of approval from the crowd. Every completed exercise resulted in a standing ovation. Salzman now loves playing so much that he carries his cello everywhere, even on book tours, and practices three times a day.

How can you act as though you're successful when you don't really feel it? Pretend and the feelings will follow. What if you really are not that good yet? It doesn't matter. You are developing into an accomplished writer, learning as you go.

Tom Watson, Sr., the founder of IBM, explained the secret of his company's success: before he began building the company he created a mental picture of how it would look when it was done. He asked himself how the company would operate when it was functioning successfully, and ran it that way from the very beginning. To become a great company, IBM had to act like a great company right from the start.

Likewise, to become a great writer you need to act like a great writer. That doesn't mean being temperamental or demanding. It means treating yourself with respect and understanding that you are constantly learning and that solving problems is part of the task. Give yourself time to work. Give yourself time to wander in the woods and reflect. As a successful writer, you need these things and must find ways to live like the artist you wish to become.

You might have a preconceived notion about how a successful writer functions, putting in a certain number of hours every day—time you just don't seem to have. Forget about how other people have done it. You are creating success out of your own particular circumstances and temperament. You may not be able to get up at 5 A.M. and spend eight hours at your desk. You may only be able to write for an hour after the kids are in bed. You may only write on weekends or at lunch breaks. But you are developing in your own way. Just take yourself seriously and trust that the things that make you different will work to your advantage.

If, for instance, you have been thinking that as a housewife you can never really be a successful writer, imagine the press praising you as someone who painted a marvelous portrait of a woman who stayed home to raise her children. If fears that you are too old to make a name for yourself have stopped you from trying, picture the reviews saying, "At last, a writer who began late in life!"

Mystery writer Elmore Leonard finally made it to literary stardom with a marketing campaign that touted him as "an overnight success after twenty years." Imagine your handicaps as the "hook" for future publicity. Make up a headline (He Could Never Hold A Job! She Wrote While Doing Laundry!) and post it over your desk for inspiration.

Renowned psychologist Victor Frankl, author of *Man's Search for Meaning*, was able to survive the horror of Nazi labor camps by constantly imagining himself at a lectern, talking to a large audience about the psychology of concentration camp victims, and recounting the suffering he had witnessed.

Take a few minutes to imagine a future in which you have become the writer you've always wanted to be. You are living the way you want to live in a place filled with things that you love. You have created work of which you are proud. Imagine this future you, sitting somewhere comfortable and looking back on this day when you were still struggling. Let this future you reassure the present you that everything will work out. That you are not alone in the struggle. Better times do lie ahead. All the difficulties and insecurities you experienced over the years were simply part of the process.

Take a look at your workspace. This is the place where wonderful writing begins. It may be too messy, it may be too neat, but it is a sanctified space and you should love it.

When you look back from a successful future, you can see rejections with a sense of humor and perspective. You can understand that because a publisher did not like a piece of work didn't necessarily mean it wasn't any good, but simply that it was not appropriate for that particular person at that particular time. Or it may turn out that the piece really wasn't good enough, that you still needed to learn some things—about character development or description or narrative thrust—but you were learning by doing.

Your early writing efforts help you develop and are essential to achieving later success.

If you are working on a project, go to that project now, acting like a successful writer. Or use the next fifteen minutes to write from the future.

Imagine you are being interviewed for the *Paris Review* "Writers at Work" series. Tell the interviewer what it was like for you in the beginning when you were struggling to find your way. Talk about the hardships you endured and how you overcame them. Write about the way you dealt with your limitations. Describe your strengths and what you had to do to improve them. When you have finished this exercise, you will know what you need to do next. Then, with an attitude of humility and pride, get to work.

Ask yourself what success would look like for one, or more, of your characters. How does this character define success? What is his idea of failure? Where does she think she is now? Write a scene in which one of your characters experiences his or her version of success. This person may never achieve that vision, but it will be valuable for you to know what it looks, tastes, smells, and feels like. Do this with a minor character as well as with a major character. Or create a scene in which one character describes a moment of triumph to another.

find the Music

Before Edgar Award–winning writer Sharon McCrumb (*She Walks These Hills*) begins a novel, she creates a soundtrack for the book, finding music to fit each character and recording it on tape. She might assign a Scottish folk ballad to an escaping convict or a country western tune to a lonely sheriff. McCrumb listens to this tape when she's driving in her car and steeps herself in a character's music when she's preparing to write his or her scene.

You might want to try McCrumb's trick and look for a piece of music that captures the essence of a character. Or choose two pieces, one dramatically different from the other. You may discover that besides country western, your sheriff also has a secret passion for opera, or that your uptight schoolteacher loves not only harpsichord sonatas, but Mississippi blues as well.

"When I'm writing, any sound just jangles," says writer/illustrator Art Speigelman, "but when I'm drawing I start by listening to music." While working on his Pulitzer Prize–winning Holocaust memoir *Maus*, Speigelman listened to music from the '20s and '30s—the kind played in Betty Boop cartoons. He played tapes of the German comedian harmonists so often that his wife Françoise "was ready to drive me out of the house with my tape recorder, never to darken the door again."

If you are writing about a specific period, spend time listening to music from that era. If you are writing about a foreign place, immerse yourself in the sounds of that world. You might enjoy hearing the music while you work or might prefer to listen during your off time.

Joseph Heller often plays Bach choral music when he writes. "It overcomes those noises that might distract me—a leaking faucet, my daughter's rock music . . . someone else's radio across the courtyard."

Amy Tan also writes to music. "I don't actually listen to it. But it blocks out the rest of my consciousness so that I can enter another world." While writing *The Hundred Secret Senses,* she listened to movie soundtracks.

Short story writer Harlan Ellison uses the film scores composed by Ennio Morricone (such as *The Good, The Bad and The Ugly* or *A Fistful of Dollars)* to help loosen his imagination. Children's poet Jack Prelutsky prefers writing to Mozart and Brahms while Stephen King likes rock and roll. King bought himself a radio station in Bangor, Maine, so he could have heavy metal music available any time of day.

For three years, whenever she felt a poem coming on, Anne Sexton played a recording of "Bachianas Brasilieras" by Hector Villa Lobos. She considered this her magic tune.

Some authors cannot tolerate music when they work. "The actual process of writing demands complete, noiseless privacy," says novelist William Styron. "A baby howling two blocks away will drive me nuts." But he considers music essential to his creative life. In fact he credits the Brahms alto rhapsody with saving him from suicide. "The sound . . . pierced my heart like a dagger and in a flood of swift recollection I thought of all the joys the house had known: the children who had rushed through its rooms, the festivals, the

more often. In this way he strengthened her support system so that readers could see her lovingly reflected in these people's eyes. "She was weak before," he explained, "so I put these buttresses around to keep her upright."

Whenever you write a story, an essay, a screenplay, or a song, you are building an edifice—a structure within which emotions and ideas can live. You are creating a place that other people can visit. It may serve as a shrine, an information booth, a world.

What kind of structure are you erecting to convey your idea or contain your story? Are you building an ornate palace to dazzle your readers or a cozy cottage where they can enjoy a relaxing vacation? Write down what you'd like your reader to experience: Comfort? Amazement? Fear? Then describe the most suitable structure for acheiving that effect.

As I thought about the structure of *The Observation Deck*, I realized that it is not an ordinary building. It is a series of modular units that can be rearranged like the walls of a museum show. It contains fifty doorways through which you can enter. It is also an observation deck like the Eiffel Tower, designed to help you see things from a new perspective. You can climb very high to get an overview of your process, but if your head has been in the clouds too long, there are elevators designed to bring you back to level ground.

Franz Kafka clearly built *The Metamorphosis* like a claustrophobic room and "The Trial" like a labyrinth of bureacratic corridors. Gloria Naylor's *Women of Brewster Place* is constructed like a housing project, with many people living packed-in, close together. Each story is a separate apartment and yet, in their concerns for safety and the love they all share, the residents are connected by common walls and pathways.

As you think architecturally about your own writing, explore how you can make the entrances to your work more inviting. How can you make it easier for them to get in? Are there places where your readers can rest? Do you want to keep them constantly moving, looking for a treasure at the end the story, or do you want them to linger a while in every room? Do you want them to be uncomfortable or intrigued when they reach certain points, so they continue turning the pages?

As you walk down the street, notice the buildings that make up your world. Pay attention to windows, lobbies, doors. Think about how people get from one level to another. Stairways? Elevators? Ramps or slides? How do you take readers from one level to the next? Think about how you ventilate your story. Is the tone fairly cool or does it heat up? Who or what can you bring in to provide a welcome breath of fresh air? What danger or drama might you introduce to raise the temperature of a scene?

Ken Follett discovered the power of structure when he was beginning his eleventh book, *The Eye of the Needle*. Agent/editor Al Zuckerman had complained that his previous books had been "too thin," so Follett devised a structure to help himself develop each scene more fully. Each chapter would be ten typewritten pages long. The book would be divided into six sections, each consisting of six chapters which alternated point of view in a regular pattern. First the German spy, Faber, then the British spies, Godliman and Bloggs, then the innocent couple, David and Lucy, back to Godliman and Bloggs, then again to the David and Lucy. The sixth chapter of each section would be shorter and focus on the world outside of the story. "The regular structure" said Follett, "was a discipline for me so I would not just develop the main strands of the story but show the parallel developments for each group of characters. . . . It was for my own benefit, to make sure I didn't cut to the chase too quickly."

The result was that someone reading the book could have the same feeling he or she might have when walking through a cathedral with its rhythmic pattern of pillars, windows, and bays.

Is there a structure you might design to help you avoid a bad writing habit? Can you set some boundaries, or adopt a pattern that will help you know when each section is done?

If you are writing a nonfiction piece about an object or a concept, think about the architecture of that thing or idea. Find the shape that best describes it. Are you talking about a food pyramid? A circle of influence? The four quadrants of a square? Play with the visual imagery and see if it helps you better explain your work.

When I first began working on this project, I asked Edgar Award–winning mystery writer Julie Smith *(New Orleans Mourning)* what she does to find inspiration. She confessed that she listens to other people's conversations. In cafes, on elevators, in the street. This is how she learns the rhythms, the jargon, the concerns of people she would not otherwise understand. Working on a scene involving runaways, she ventured down to Berkeley's Telegraph Avenue and eavesdropped on a

Eavesdrop

group of pierced, tattooed teenagers sporting Mohawk haircuts and spiked dog collars. As she listened to their conversations she began to see them, not as the punks she'd first imagined, but as kids trying to look tough in a difficult world.

Many writers are notorious eavesdroppers. Eudora Welty explained the practice, saying, "In the South, everybody stays busy talking all the time—they're not sorry for you to overhear their tales. I don't feel, in helping myself, I ever did anything underhanded. I was helping out!" F. Scott Fitzgerald kept a notebook in which he recorded "overheard conversations" as well as "nonsense and stray phrases."

153

When Nelson Algren, author of *The Man with a Golden Arm*, was asked how he developed his style, he replied, "The only thing I've consciously tried to do was put myself in a position to hear the people I wanted to hear talk, talk." For seven years he frequented police lineups—ostensibly searching for a mugger—listening to conversations among the criminals and cops.

When you're waiting in line, have pen and paper with you so you can jot down odd things you overhear. Play with a phrase when you get home and see where it leads you. Donald Katz, the National Book Award–winning author of *Home Fires*, *The Big Store*, and *Just Do It*, says he finds nothing more difficult than facing a blank page, so he collects phrases with which to improvise. When interviewing someone, he jots down statements that have a certain charge or musical ring and then, when he gets back to his desk, he brainstorms using those phrases. Katz gets many of his best ideas when he mis-hears what other people say.

"I do not think you can transfer anything, as it is spoken, onto the page and have it come out at all convincingly," said Eudora Welty to interviewer Bill Ferris. "It has to be absolutely rewritten on the page from the way it happens, *but if you didn't know how it happened, you couldn't start*."

Science fiction writer Dan Simmons suggests that you take fifteen minutes to eavesdrop on a conversation, writing down every word you hear. Or tape record an interaction and type it up word-for-word. When you reread your transcription, you will find it full of repetition, unfinished thoughts, nonsequiturs. Having demonstrated to yourself the disjointed nature of real conversation, you can now edit the transcript down to one or two pages. Simmons recommends that you read some well-written dialogue–Mark Twain, Ernest Hemingway, Elmore Leonard–before you start editing, to learn how to make conversation work on the page.

Eudora Welty said that dialogue is action. "Dialogue has to show not only something about the speaker that is its own revelation, but also maybe something about the speaker that he doesn't know but the other speaker does know. You've got to show a two-way revelation between speaker and listener."

For James Jones, author of *From Here to Eternity*, "conversation is more often likely to be an attempt at deliberate evasion, deliberate confusion, rather than communication." Short story writer Raymond Carver was a master at demonstrating this. Pay attention to what is *not* said in a conversation. Reread your transcript and look for the hidden agenda each speaker is trying to further. If a man is trying to seduce a woman, what techniques is he using? Flattery? Boasting? Subtly denigrating his rival? What are the indirect techniques the salesman uses? Does he try to make the buyer feel he's behind the times? Drop names of other famous clients? Ask questions to establish rapport?

If you are writing about a particular subculture, find it locally and go eavesdrop, with pen and paper ready. Visit an old folks home, a gambling den, or an exclusive club. Pay attention to what the patrons are talking about. Notice the rhythms, the jargon, the secret codes. Then see if you can construct a scene that captures what you've learned. Write an interaction between patient and nurse over feeding time. Or a student-teacher confrontation regarding a missed assignment. Remember what is not said is as important as what is said, and that conversation is often indirect.

To stretch your imagination, try the game played by the ten-year-old heroine of Louise Fitzhugh's *Harriet the Spy*. Sipping an egg cream at her favorite luncheonette, Harriet would "let the voices from the tables behind her float over her head" and try to guess what each person looked like from his or her conversation. You may be surprised at the accuracy of your guesses, or you may discover that you need to listen more carefully for clues regarding age, class, and appearance.

While you are going about your daily tasks, take note of the various ways people say good-bye. Is it "See you later"? "Gotta go"? Or "Would you please excuse me"? Notice the different ways people say "I'm sorry."

You might also want to take a conversation you have already written or found in someone else's work and recast it with very different participants. Rewrite a scene from *Romeo and Juliet* as a conversation between two immigrants, or between a teacher and an attractive student. You will have to make each character specific—with particular needs and histories—and create well-defined circumstances to make the conversation seem real.

"How you juxtapose events can tie you up," said Phillip Roth. "Rearranging the sequence can free you suddenly to streak to the finish line." Roth was struggling to complete *Zuckerman Unbound* when he recognized a structural flaw. He needed to move the death of his hero's father—which originally occurred before the book began—to the end of the book, where it could serve as the culmination, rather than the instigation, of events.

Blaise Pascal, the seventeenth-century

Rearrange

French philosopher, once said, "The last thing you know when writing a book is what to put first." This can be true even when your inspiration comes from a brilliant opening line.

Joseph Heller was sitting on his deck worrying about his writing career when into his head popped, "In the office in which I work, there are four people of whom I am afraid." He thought this would make a great opening for a novel; so began *Something Happened.* Over time this opening was replaced by "I get the willies when I see closed doors," and the first section was moved to the second part of the book.

The opening chapter of *Midnight in the Garden of Good and Evil* was originally chapter nine. Chapter one became chapter two when John Berendt realized that he couldn't wait until the middle of the book to introduce the murderer, Jim Williams.

Truman Capote began writing *Answered Prayers* with what he thought would be the last chapter. He then wrote the first, fifth, and seventh chapters, claiming he was able to keep the threads of plot straight only because he knew how each story ended in real life.

Phillip Roth told the *Paris Review*, "For all I know I am beginning with the ending. My page one can wind up a year later as page two hundred, if it's around at all."

If you don't know where to begin, start anywhere. Start in the middle of an argument. Or start with your characters lost in a maze. If you're stuck not knowing what happens next, skip to a later scene. You do not have to work in sequence. Woody Allen, Anthony Burgess, and Ed McBain have all said they can only start at the beginning and work clear through, but Katherine Anne Porter and Toni Morrison both start their books at the end. Porter says, "I always write my last line, my last paragraph, my last page first." Morrison echoes with "I always know the endings; that's where I begin."

Some authors know neither the beginning nor the ending. Long after Sue Bender had returned from living with the Amish, she heard a voice inside saying, "Now it's time to tell the story." Lacking confidence that she could write, Bender began by simply scribbling notes on scraps of paper. After she'd accumulated quite a pile, she spread the papers out on the floor and tried to make sense of them. For several years she moved these scraps around on the rug until she began to see them as patches from which she could stitch a quilt. She chose the simplest pattern, the nine patch, to organize her story, and from this emerged *Plain and Simple: A Woman's Journey to the Amish*.

Even if you work on a computer with cut-and-paste functions, you might find it helpful to print out your text and manually rearrange things. Eudora Welty worked with scissors and push pins, cutting and rearranging pieces until a story felt right.

If you are working on a speech or a research paper, there is nothing better than working with index cards. You can make notes directly onto the cards, arrange them by topic, and then create your structure.

Vladimir Nabakov used to compose his novels on index cards. He would copy, expand, and rearrange them until the story coalesced. In writing *The Observation Deck,* I often wrote several rough drafts, then copied the best ideas and anecdotes onto index cards and used them to compose the finished text.

Sometimes a more complex structure is not as effective as a straightforward one. When Melody Ermachild was writing *Altars in the Street,* she thought she'd open with the murder that took place in front of her house. After all, the book had come about because an agent had read her essay on the murder in *Sierra* magazine. She figured she'd start with the image from her essay and work backwards. But during the final days before the book was due, she phoned her friend Barbara Selfridge in a panic, needing help. The two of them laid the manuscript on the dining room table and moved the chapters around until Barbara exclaimed, "Let the story build. Make it chronological." She rearranged the text into a standard narrative form and it worked.

If you normally work out of sequence, try telling a story from start to finish. If you usually write straightforward narrative, tell the story backwards.